Men of Wisdom

MUḤAMMAD

AND THE ISLAMIC TRADITION

By

ÉMILE DERMENGHEM

Translated from the French by
JEAN M. WATT

NEW YORK
HARPER & BROTHERS

LONDON
LONGMANS

CONTENTS

MUHAMMAD

THE ISLAMIC TRADITION

TEXTS

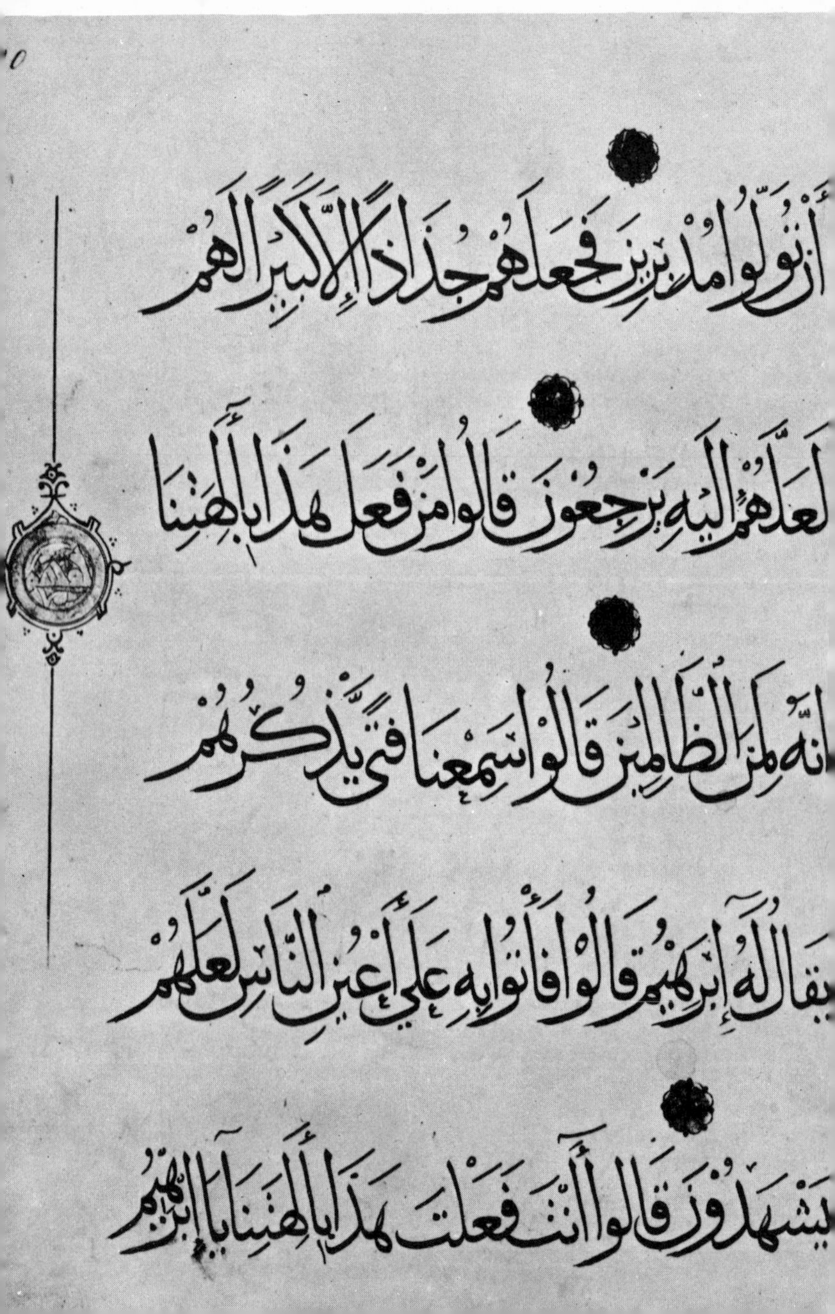

أن تولوا مدبرين فجعلهم جذاذا إلا كبيرا لهم

لعلهم إليه يرجعون قالوا من فعل هذا بآلهتنا

إنه لمن الظالمين قالوا سمعنا فتى يذكرهم

يقال له إبرهيم قالوا فأتوا به على أعين الناس لعلهم

يشهدون قالوا أأنت فعلت هذا بآلهتنا يا إبرهيم

THE SOURCES

In 622 Muḥammad emigrated from Mecca to Medina, where he died in 632. These two dates, and those of the chief intervening events, are certain; but those prior to 622 are more dubious. The date of the Prophet's birth and that of his first revelation can only be given approximately, and the first two-thirds of his life are known only in broad outline. The influences to which he was subjected and the origins of the religious crisis which was to have such wide repercussions in history can only be glimpsed. In spite of all this, Muḥammad is a historical person whose life cannot be relegated to mythology; the legendary elements in this life have been added by the zeal of later writers, but they can be discarded.

The fundamental source for the life is the Qur'ān. It is often allusive, but it is at least authentic. It is a series of revelations referring to contemporary events which came to Muḥammad during a period of twenty years. In it one finds not only doctrine, preaching and legislation, but also judgements on the various happenings, and appropriate exhortations.

We must be careful when dealing with the detailed information given about various verses by the commentators. They were obviously at pains to fill in the gaps and to elucidate the passages, but they were sometimes overscrupulous and did not hesitate to give several versions if occasion demanded, even when this might be awkward.

Another source, rich but less reliable, is the Traditions, contained in the collections of the *ḥadīth*. They are valuable since they reproduce all that was known of the sayings and actions of the Prophet and his Companions. Each has a chain of witnesses and reporters, and they include the most minute details and the slightest variants. They took all this trouble to preserve the teaching and example of 'the best model'.

Page from a 14th century Qur'an.

The imagination is stirred by this attempt, ambitious yet dangerous, to establish from the life of a small group of men in a hidden corner of Arabia in the seventh century, the sources of dogma, morals, ritual, politics, economics, hygiene and jurisprudence for a community which aimed at becoming universal. So it came about that different points of view, different schools and different powers searched in this material to find—or to fabricate—arguments and weapons.

Most of the authors of the great collections, especially Bukhāri and Muslim, undoubtedly had a genuinely critical outlook. Every hadīth which supports a tendentious thesis or favours the claims of a political party, of a dynasty, or of a theological, moral or legal school, must be treated with reserve. But one may well think that this effort to preserve the memory of a man who lived in the full light of history was not altogether in vain. Those traditions which are not biographically exact have a truthfulness of another sort; they have contributed to the formation of the Islamic tradition. In any case, it is fortunate for this tradition that there are contradictions in it and various shades of meaning. If it were not for these, how could it fail to be rigid and inflexible?

The third source is the *sīrah*, the biographies constructed by historians from the eighth century onwards. They are based on the Qur'ān and the hadith, but are given the form of a chronological and coherent story. We have here made use chiefly of the *Sīrat-ar-Rasūl*, the Life of the Prophet, by Ibn Hishām, who died in 834—without doubt the oldest and best life of Muḥammad. It summarizes and draws on a great lost work of Ibn Isḥāq. Later biographers are at once less complete, less direct and less critical. There is a lack, to put it plainly, of accounts from other sources with which to make comparisons. The Byzantine historians hardly dealt with Arabia. Some background information is to be gained from the Arabic literary sources which furnished Lammens with so much material and enabled him to describe in detail the state of the country and the 'cradle of Islam'. They also have many facts of importance for ethnography and comparative religion.

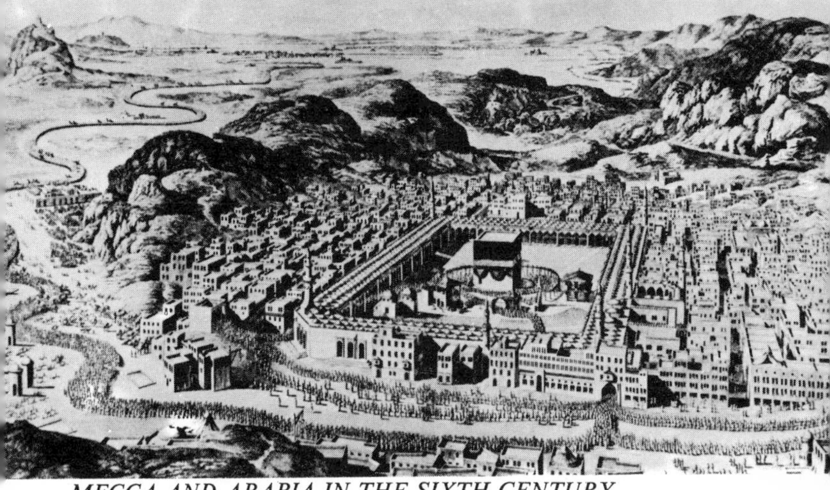

Mecca in the 18th century. (Engraving by D'Ohson, 1790)

MECCA AND ARABIA IN THE SIXTH CENTURY

Tradition has it that Muḥammad was born in the Year of the Elephant. This was the year when Abraham the Abyssinian viceroy of the Yemen made an unsuccessful expedition against Mecca, which, had it succeeded, might have won over the entire Ḥijāz to monophysite Christianity. This Year of the Elephant must be prior to 572, and is doubtless 571. With its passion for symmetry, tradition dates Muḥammad's prophetic mission from the time he was forty, and reckons his preaching period at Mecca and the final period at Medina each as ten years. Some make his age sixty-three or sixty-five. His birth would then fall between 567 and 572, the most likely date being 571, which would place the beginning of his mission at approximately 612.

The name Muḥammad was either the name given him at birth or else a nickname meaning the Praised One. He was also known for a long time as Abu'l-Qāsim, an honorific name or *kunyah* meaning 'the father of al-Qāsim'. Mecca was his birth-place, and his mother was Āminah, whose husband had just died prematurely. His paternal grandfather was 'Abd al-Muṭṭalib of the clan of Hāshim, whose family had the privilege of distributing to the pilgrims the sacred water from the well Zamzam.

Mecca, situated as it was in a barren valley but at the junction of the routes leading from South Arabia to Damascus and to Mesopotamia, gained its livelihood from commerce and from the pilgrimage to the Ka'bah. This was a cube of masonry surrounded by idols, into a corner of which was built the Black Stone.

In Mecca a large Arab tribe, the Quraish, including the clans of the Banu Umayyah, the Banu Makhzūm and the Banu Hāshim, had established itself and had formed a small oligarchical republic of merchants with a council of notables (the *mala*'). In the level part of the town lay the aristocratic quarter (called the Bathā'), and the streets sloping towards the valleys between the hills were inhabited by the poorer people. The suburbs were filled with artisan slaves, adventurers, refugees, carriers, money-changers, 'metics', a few Christians, taverns and singing-women who lay in wait for bedouin and camel-drivers.

The large seasonal caravans were outstanding events; one went to the Yemen in winter, the other towards Syria in summer. Financed by the fortunes of the wealthy and by the small banks, thanks to an ingenious credit system, they bore northwards not only dates from the Ḥijāz and incense from the Yemen, but precious stones from India and silks from China; they carried cotton-goods, corn and oil. Two or three hundred men accompanied these precious wares loaded on two or three thousand camels. One can understand that their departure and still more their arrival took place amid a general fever of excitement and all sorts of eager speculations.

The Ka'bah at Mecca. (18*th century miniature*)

The other source of revenues and prestige which helped to maintain the Quraishites in this unfriendly spot was the holy Ka'bah. The Arabs did not reject out of hand the idea of a God who was the supreme Creator, but they were only mildly concerned with this Allāh. Their worship ranged from numerous divinities, who might be his sons or his daughters, to the jinn (or genies), who inspired soothsayers and poets, and tormented travellers and sick people, and to the carved stones which embodied for them the vague 'holy' and over which they poured blood and oil.

The Ka'bah, a cubical structure

exposed to the sky, with the sacred Black Stone in a corner, stood in the middle of a large open square, where there was also another sacred stone, the *maqām* of Abraham, and the well of Zamzam. Idols of unhewn or rudely sculptured stone surrounded the temple, around which was performed the essential rite of *ṭawāf*, a sevenfold circumambulation in a counter-clockwise direction. The pilgrimage was completed by visits to other holy sites, al-Ṣafa and al-Marwah in the town, and Muzdalifah, Minā and ʻArafāt in the neighbourhood. Four sacred months established a sort of truce of God, interrupting for the benefit of pilgrimage and commerce, the traditional cycle of small wars. Commerce was also stimulated by large annual fairs in the region, for example, the fair of ʻUkāẓ, where orators and poets competed.

It is obvious that anyone who tried to attack this clerical plutocracy and who sought to fight the profiteering and speculation, or to proclaim the primacy of the Other World and forbid all idolatrous worship, would get a cold reception. The extraordinary destiny of Muḥammad was to be the leader in all these attacks, and to impose as supreme law, above tribal customs, the Word of God which he had received in states of trance. He failed at first in his

Prayers round the Kaʻbah. (*Modern popular picture, Algeria*)

homeland. Then he left it to found a state in a little oasis of the Ḥijāz. Finally he returned as conqueror. His victory was the triumph of the One True God. He retained the pilgrimage as part of his restoration of the 'religion of Abraham'. In this way he formed a spiritual and temporal community which set out from these early beginnings to undertake the conquest of the world.

JEWS AND CHRISTIANS

Arabia, besides its polytheistic community, also included some Jews and Christians among its peoples. Prosperous and influential Jewish communities were to be found at Yathrib (Medina), at Khaibar, and in the northern oases. In the south of Arabia during the sixth century the two great religions had disputed the Yemen. Dhu Nuwās had tried to impose Judaism by force on Najrān, but was overthrown by an Abyssinian invasion, possibly instigated by the Byzantine emperor. It was from this land of the Yemen, where Abyssinian monophysite influence was strong, that Abraham's expedition had set out. His reverse provoked an offensive by the Mazdeans (Zoroastrians) of Persia, who routed the Abyssinians.

In the north and north-east of Arabia some large nomadic tribes, which the caravans from Mecca met when they went to Bostra or to Hira, were Christian, mostly Nestorian. Among them were the Ghassānids (vassals of the Byzantines), the Lakhmids, the Taghlibites and the Banu Kalb. The famous poets, Imru' al-Qais, Nābighah Dhubyāni and Ṭarafa, were Christians. At Mecca itself there were Christians in plenty, though they were often foreigners. They included Abyssinian slaves (some perhaps mercenaries), artisans (who might be either slaves or freedmen), Syrian business men, and doctors. There were also some very mysterious people, the *ḥanīfs*, who were only few in number, but were the exponents (according to the Qur'ān and the Traditions) of the pure monotheism of Abraham, which had preceded the Mosaic religion and Christianity. Some accounts depict them as anxious spirits, travellers in search of truth. Certain of them differed very little from Christians, and some were converted voluntarily to Christianity, as, for example, Waraqah, the cousin of Muhammad's wife Khadījah. Blachère is tempted to group them with the Manichaeans. Manichaean dualism, whether Christian or Mazdean-Persian, had spread widely in Arabia. When I published a life of Muḥammad beginning with the story of Salmān the Persian (or the man from Fars), an Indian Parsee wrote me that he had quite understood what I had tried to suggest. This was not in fact the case; I had had nothing at the back of my mind. I had however been struck by the importance of this somewhat mysterious person who counselled the Prophet during the campaign of the Ditch, and who had sufficient authority to intervene in the quarrels of the great Companions. He it was who came to play so great a part in the gnosis of the Ismā'ilis and the Nusairis, and who is almost deified by certain sects at the side of Muḥammad and 'Ali.

Thus it will be seen that the influences at work on Muḥammad's conscious thought were many and complex. There are more intermingling currents than the historians can distinguish. Nor is there any reason to minimize the rôle played by inspiration; for it is not opposed to Tradition but takes it as its material and gives life to various aspects of it.

Muḥammad is most certainly a prophet in the Semitic and Biblical tradition; he is an inspired poet, with soul aflame, and an absolutely fearless heart. He had his share not only of human greatness but also of human foibles. He was a leader and a fighter, preaching Holy War of the kind to be found throughout the Books of Exodus, Judges and Kings, but at the same time proclaiming some of the most striking religious truths. In common with the Jews he has a rigid monotheism, and also an acute realization of the revelation of a God who is both personal and transcendant, of a 'God with us' who is preoccupied with His chosen people. He has an indestructible belief in the final triumph of justice. Especially at the beginning, however, he inclined much more to the Christian view. Jesus was acclaimed by him as the Messiah, and as the Word and Spirit of God. He also believed in the Virgin Birth and the Immaculate Conception of Mary. He repeatedly stressed the fact of the Resurrection and his belief in Antichrist, the Last Judgement and Eternal Life. He knew some Christians but they were probably very ignorant and far removed from the centres of orthodoxy. He had evidently heard oral versions of various stories from the Old and New Testaments, from the Talmud and apocryphal writings, without having access to the texts himself. In the intense religious crisis which overtook him round about the age of forty, he attacked pagan materialism. Knowing that there was something but unable to understand it, he appealed directly, from the bottom of his conscious and unconscious mind, to Reality. His appeal was answered. A book came down from Heaven one night into his heart. He spent most of the remainder of his life receiving, from day to day, in states of trance, fragments from this 'mother of the Book' (Qur'ān xiii, 39), that is, from the eternal prototype guarded by the angels in highest Heaven (Qur'ān lxxx, 13–15). But in its passage from the Absolute into the relative world of the period from 612 (roughly) to 632, this eternal Word reflected the preoccupations of its transmitter and those of his community. It was alike revolutionary, touching, moving and sometimes offensive. It shows us, side by side and as if on the same level, the most beautiful religious and mystic truths, political and moral rules that were precise but often brief and fragmentary, revelations about the public and private life of the Prophet and his loves. It contains, too, attacks on his adversaries and exhortations to endure patiently and to take part in the holy war, and also includes imaginary pictures of the end of the world, of Paradise and of Hell. The whole was in a form so striking, that Muḥammad saw in it the only miracle to prove the authenticity of his mission as prophet. The 'inimitability' of the Qur'ān became like a dogma; the psalmody of any of its verses reflecting the uncreated Word may be used in the ritual prayer and is the 'true' sacrament of Islam.

Until now, the Arabs had not had easy access to revealed truth. Here they were being given a revelation to warn 'the Mother of Cities' (Mecca) and 'those round about her' of final doom. The whole is in a clear Arabic tongue (Qur'ān xlii, 5; vi, 92, 157; xx, 112). It was a Revelation confirming all previous revelations. For all the prophets proclaimed the same religion and it was not fitting to make a distinction between them. Muḥammad, the *ummi* prophet, the prophet sent to Gentiles, followed on and tried to rally his fellow townsmen. But difficulties presented themselves, and events took it upon themselves to produce something out of these difficulties. A prophet of the Arabs? A prophet of the last days? The last of the prophets? The greatest prophet? The prophet who was to replace all others and be supreme for all time? There is a delicate point here for all religious revolutions; each one supersedes the previous one but it does not want to be superseded in its turn. Such an attitude is no doubt exoterically necessary.

For the Jews, revelation stops at the Old Testament, for the Christians at the Apocalypse, for the Muslims at the 114 suras of the Qur'ān. Note each time that the Qur'ān declares very wisely that God will Himself at the Last Day throw light on the problems under discussion (Qur'ān v, 53; xxii, 17). On the other hand, various sects have emerged from Islam, such as the Aḥmadiyah movement and Bahaism, which claim to have succeeded in receiving revelations later than the Qur'ān.

Example of Design in Calligraphy:
'To God be praise and thanks!'

The birth of Muhammad. (Jami' at-Tawarikh, University of Edinburgh, Arabic and Persian mss., no. 20, f. 42a)

MUHAMMAD'S YOUTH

Āminah, Muḥammad's mother, was a poor young widow. The summer in Mecca threatened to be a trying one. 'Abd al-Muṭṭalib, the child's grandfather, gave him to a wet-nurse, Ḥalīmah, a bedouin woman of the tribe of Banu Sa'd. He spent his first years with her in the mountainous region near Ṭā'if, looking after the flocks with his foster-brother, for, as he said later, every prophet was in his youth a shepherd. The story is told how one day his companion saw two angels throw down the young Muḥammad, open his chest and take out of his heart a black clot. This legend is one of those cases where it is easy to cut away something from the sīraḥ.

It is based on the literal interpretation of a Qur'ānic verse ('Have We not opened thy breast, and eased thee of thy burden, which overwhelmed thee?'—xciv, 1–3), and this verse can easily be understood metaphorically as saying that the Prophet has passed from misfortune to happiness, from agony of mind to faith, and from ignorance to truth. Though this is a legend based on a false meaning, it has its importance, because it signifies that it was not until he was four or five years old that the Prophet was purified from the original sin, from which only Jesus and Mary have been exempt since birth. The legend enters also into the mystical cycle of the 'purification of the heart'.

Āminah died shortly after the return of her son. He was taken care of by his grandfather who died when he was about eight. He was then brought up by his uncle, Abu Ṭālib, who does not seem to have given him very advanced instruction, but doubtless took him to Bostra in Syria, where a Nestorian monk, Baḥirā, is said to have foretold his call to be a prophet. This last point is merely an attempt to give evidence for his prophethood, yet one can well imagine that on his travels in the north the young man was struck, not only by the magnificence of the Byzantines, but by the magic of the Land of the prophets, that Land where Abraham had lived, where there had 'come down' (been revealed) the Torah of Moses, the Zabūr (Psalms) of David, and the Injīl (Evangel, Gospel) of Jesus. The virtues of Christian monks, too, are extolled in the Qur'ān (v, 85).

Muḥammad ended by entering the service of a rich widow, Khadījah, conducting her caravans, becoming her steward, then her husband. This marriage was remarkably happy. This man, who was later to have a number of wives, was faithful for more than twenty years to a woman older than himself. It was not merely ties of gratitude which bound him to her; she could understand him and comfort him in the rather frightening crisis when the revelations began to come to him and trials followed. By her he had two or three sons who died at an early age and four daughters, Zainab, Ruqaiyah, Umm Kulthūm and Fāṭimah (the last-mentioned being the only one who had descendants). He adopted, besides, Zaid ibn Ḥārithah of the Banu Kalb, enslaved in a desert raid and eventually freed by Muḥammad.

Muhammad as a youth greeted by the monk Bahira.
(*University of Edinburgh, Arabic and Persian mss., no.* 20, *f.* 43*b*)

THE PROPHET'S CALL

About his fortieth year, perhaps about 610–612, Muḥammad gave himself over to ascetic practices quite foreign to paganism, withdrawing into the mountains to pray and meditate, after having given away a considerable amount as alms.

Overwhelmed doubtless as much by the splendour of the world as by man's lack of understanding, he buried himself in contemplation before the multitudes of stars to be seen in the desert on a summer's night. The Qur'ān was soon to take them as witnesses of the infinite power of a God who was both Creator and Judge.

> I swear by the heaven and the night-star!
> Who shall make thee know what the night-star is?
> It is the star of piercing brightness. . . . (lxxxvi)
> I swear by the heaven adorned with constellations! (lxxxvi)
> By the sun and its rising brightness! . . .
> By the heaven and Him who built it!
> By the earth and Him who spread it!
> By the Soul! . . .
> Blessed is he who hath purified it!
> Wretched is he who hath corrupted it! (xci)

The Creator has loaded man with benefits. He has created him 'from a clot of blood' (the embryo). He has fashioned him 'from clay like a potter's vessel'. He has provided the sun for his light, the moon to guide his caravan by night, beasts of burden to carry him, and seas on which to sail his fleets (lv, xvi). He has sent him prophets to guide him in the narrow way and sacred books to instruct him where he was ignorant. All this is very serious: the benefactor will seek a reckoning.

The hour approacheth. The moon hath been split. (liv)
When the sun shall be darkened,
When the stars shall fall,
When the mountains shall be demolished. . . .
When Hell shall burn fiercely,
When Paradise shall be brought near,
Every soul shall know what it hath wrought. (lxxxi)

The heathen are plunged in darkness and do not even know that the light exists, wrapped up as they are in their selfishness and wordly cares. Muḥammad himself trembled in agony and called for a guide. It was then that the world-shaking fact was born. A messenger was sent to him with the Truth. The Qur'ān mentions two great visions of one whom he later identified as the angel Jibrā'il (Gabriel).

By the star when it setteth!
Your companion erreth not . . . .
It is no other than a Revelation which hath been revealed unto Him,
It hath been taught to him by an angel mighty in power,
Endued with understanding. He appeared in majesty
When he was in the highest horizon,
Then he drew near and remained suspended
At a distance of two bows' length or nearer,
Then he revealed to his servant what he revealed. . . .
He also saw him another time
By the lote-tree of the Boundary
Near which is the Garden of eternal abode,
When there covered the lote-tree what covered it.
His sight turned not aside, neither did it wander.
Truly he beheld one of the greatest signs of his Lord. (liii, 1–18)

According to the tradition and to the biographies it was a night in the last third of Ramadān, in a grotto on Mount Ḥirā', when there took place the infusion of the uncreated Word into the relative world, the 'coming down' of the Book into the heart of the Prophet (the Night of Destiny, the Blessed Night of the Qur'ān). While he was sleeping, a mysterious being, holding in his hand a roll of material covered with signs, ordered him to read (or recite, or chant). 'I do not know how to read,' said Muḥammad. 'Read,' the angel repeated again twice, winding the material round the neck of the sleeper. 'What shall I read?' 'Read:

Read, in the name of thy Lord who hath created,
Who hath created man from clotted blood.
Read: for thy Lord is the most beneficent.
It is he who hath taught man to use the pen.
He hath taught man what man knew not.' (xcvi)

The chosen one woke with the knowledge that a Book had 'come down' into his heart. Sight followed the dream. He left the cave (the dark grotto where light is born, as in most ancient religious traditions) and suddenly he heard himself called and greeted by the name of Messenger of Allah. He looked up and saw an enormous man standing on the horizon. Dazzled, Muḥammad turned and once again saw the angel. From every part of the heaven the angel would stand and gaze at him in silence.

He went home distraught, wanting to know if he were mad or possessed, and knelt before Khadījah, putting his head on her lap and telling her all that had happened. This good-hearted woman rose to the occasion. Although everything might make her think that her husband was ill and had gone mad, she declared her trust in him. Muḥammad was a sincere and truthful man, she urged, kind and generous; God would not permit him to be led astray by devils. He would be the prophet of his people and she would be the first person to believe in him.

Partly reassured, therefore, she went and saw her cousin, old blind Waraqah, who encouraged her in her belief; the mysterious messenger must be the same one who had spoken to Moses and the prophets.

But for the chosen one this was the end of a peaceful and honoured life. His heart was not pacified. 'We are going to reveal to you a heavy word' (lxxiii, 5). The revelation was broken off, and he passed through the dread of the 'dark night'. He started to wander among the hills, escaping by himself, not finding inspiration again in the very places where it had first come to him, almost on the verge of suicide, but always calmed and consoled by Khadījah. ('When I was poor she enriched me; when all the world abandoned me, she comforted me; when I was called a liar, she believed in me.')

But the angel speaks again.

I swear by the morning brightness,
By the night when it groweth dark,

Muhammad and the angel Gabriel.
(University of Edinburgh, Arabic and Persian mss., no. 20, *f.* 45*b)*

Thy Lord hath not forsaken thee, neither doth He hate thee.
Verily the life to come shall be better for thee than this present life.
God shall give thee wherewith thou shalt be well pleased.
Did He not find thee an orphan and hath He not sheltered thee?
Did He not find thee straying and hath He not guided thee?
Did He not find thee needy and hath He not enriched thee?
Oppress not the orphan,
Neither repulse the beggar,
But declare the goodness of thy Lord. (xciii)

For three years intimate friends and a few others accepted his mission: Khadījah, his cousin 'Ali, his adopted son Zaid, his friend and future father-in-law Abu Bakr, and his son-in-law 'Uthmān the Umayyad. Then the order came to preach openly to the Quraishites.

O prophet, publish what has come down to thee from thy Lord.
If thou doest it not, thou hast not delivered thy message. . . .
Proclaim that which thou hast been commanded without fear of the heathen,

What did he at first say to these pagans? The suras of the Qur'ān are not arranged chronologically. We only know that some belong, roughly speaking, to the Meccan period, others to the period at Medina, and that the shortest, which are last in the usual arrangement, are in general the oldest. Orientalists, especially Nöldeke, followed more recently in this respect by Blachère (and, in English, by Bell), have tried to fix them more precisely and have suggested a skilful rearrangement, though one that can only be approximate: first of all the Prophet laid stress on the call to repentance and to works of mercy and on the imminence of the Last Judgement; then on the mission of the previous prophets and the punishments undergone by those who had rejected them; then on the absolute divine Oneness, the duties of the faithful, polemics with opponents, the happenings, the vicissitudes and the organization of the community.

Grimme, at the end of last century, tended to make Muḥammad appear as a 'socialist', drawing upon the *zakāt*, the tithe given as alms, in order to equalize fortunes. This thesis hardly holds water, but it is certain that the Prophet reacted strongly to the Quraishite plutocracy, the absence of charity, and the preference given to this world's goods over the realities of the world to come.

What thinkest thou of him who seeth the Judgement as falsehood?
It is he who pusheth away the orphan,
And stirreth not up others to feed the poor. (cvii)
The emulous desire of multiplying riches employeth you
Until ye go down into the grave.
Truly hereafter shall ye know,
Yea, truly hereafter shall ye know. . . .
Verily ye shall see Hell,
Ye shall surely see it with the eye of certainty.
Then shall ye be examined concerning your pleasures. (cii)

Casanova saw in Muḥammad essentially the prophet of the end of the world (just as certain exegetes tried to portray the early Christians as imminently expecting the Second Coming). This thesis, also, is too exclusive. But it is certain that an obsessive thought of the Hour and eschatological preoccupations predominate in many of the oldest suras of the Qur'ān. It is always wise to set oneself in the prophetic perspective, which confuses the times and proclaims truths supratemporal, dynamic and metaphysical, perpetually valid.

That which ye are promised is about to come. (lxxvii)
The heathen see their punishment afar off,
But we see it nigh at hand. (lxx)
When, they ask, will this threat be accomplished, if ye speak true?
Answer, Peradventure some part of that punishment which ye desire to be hastened is already close behind you. (xxvii, 73 f.)

Many ḥadīth seem to show that Muḥammad personally envisaged the imminence of the great catastrophe, proclaiming a crack in the wall of Gog and Magog (cf. Qur'ān, xviii, 92–99). In any case the Prophet and the Hour are like two fingers of a hand. This signifies that he is essentially a warner, reminding people of Reality and the absolute certainty of Justice. Chronologically, Knowledge of the Hour is God's secret. In the meantime it is essential to have always present to one's spirit what makes the essential significance of the human soul.

Everything on earth is subject to decay.
Alone the face of thy Lord shall remain in glory and majesty. (lv, 26f.)
Whoever shall have wrought good of the weight of a grain shall see it.
Whoever shall have wrought evil of the weight of a grain shall see it likewise. (xcix, 7f.)

His lively descriptions overwhelm the faithful.

The Blow! What is the Blow?
Who shall make thee understand what the Blow is?
The day when men shall be scattered like moths,
When the mountains shall be like carded wool before the wind. (ci)
On that day man shall say, Where is a place of refuge?
By no means; there shall be no place to fly unto!
With thy Lord shall be the sure mansion of rest. (lxxv, 10–12)

THE PERSECUTIONS

But the majority of the Quraishites were sceptical, and the Prophet heard more voices raised in mockery than in approval when he proclaimed the resurrection of the body ('They say, Shall we surely be made to return to the earth after we shall have become rotten bones?' lxxix, 10f.), and when he recited the well-known descriptions of Paradise and Hell, whose material character ought not to allow us to forget that 'good-will from God shall be their most excellent reward; this will be great felicity' (ix, 73), and that the greatest joy of Paradise will be 'the greeting of peace addressed to the elect by their Lord, the Merciful'.

> They shall not hear therein any vain discourse, nor any charge of sin,
> But only the salutation, Peace! Peace! (lvi, 24f.)

Muḥammad, in order to enlarge his circle of first believers in obedience to a divine order, began by addressing the members of the Hāshimite clan. He did not even succeed in convincing his uncle Abu Ṭālib, who continued to protect him but was destined to die an unbeliever. Even in this clan he was to find one of his most violent enemies; Abu Lahab, like Abu Sufyān of the Umayyad clan, was for long to remain his most able adversary. He did not meet with much greater success when he addressed the whole of Quraish. He found his disciples chiefly among the poor, the common people of the suburbs and the slaves. The aristocracy only became more hostile, taking offence at this influence, and bringing pressure to bear on the poorer people to prevent them from being converted (xxxiv, 30–32). Hence the invectives of the Qur'ān against the rich men who commit the two great crimes:

> He believed not in the great God.
> He was not solicitous to feed the poor. (lxix, 33f.)

Then there were let loose—perhaps after a moment's hesitation and an attempt at syncretistic conciliation—virulent attacks against the gods of the Quraishites: Hubal, hidden in the Ka'bah, before whom one drew arrows from a quiver to discover one's fate, and Al-Lāt, Al-'Uzzā and Manāt, whom they regarded as the daughters of Allāh—an unthinkable aberration.

> Hath thy Lord daughters and they sons?
> Do they go so far in their false invention as to say:
> 'Allah hath begotten issue,
> That He preferred daughters to sons'? (xxxvii, 149ff.)
>
> They have set up the jinn as partners with God although He created them; in their ignorance they have falsely attributed unto Him sons and daughters. Praise be unto Him, and far be that from Him which they attribute unto Him!
>
> He, the maker of heaven and earth, how should He have issue since He hath no consort? (vi, 100f.)
>
> God hath taken no wife, nor hath He begotten any issue. (lxxii, 3.)

All this, be it remarked in passing, minimizes and qualifies the objections to the divine 'sonship' of Jesus.

The fundamental creed of Islam is formulated:

> Say: God the One!
> God alone!
> He begetteth not, neither is he begotten.
> There is not any one like unto Him. (cxii)
> God is the creator of all things; He is the One, the victorious God. (xiii, 17)

The break is complete.

> I worship not that which ye worship.
> Neither do ye worship that which I worship.
> Ye have your religion, and I my religion. (cix)

They scattered the Muslims when they went apart to pray. They drowned the voice of Muḥammad by cries or coarse songs when he tried to preach. Abu Jahl threw a sheep's placenta at the back of his neck one day when he was at prayer before the Ka'ba, but the Prophet simply got his daughter to wash him. 'Uqba spat in his face; he wiped his face calmly and then fell into a trance during which he received the verse: 'One day the sinner will bite his fingers' (xxv, 29).

When he felt most deeply discouraged revelation came to his aid, in halting verses and shaky rhymes:

Say: I fly for refuge to the Lord of the daybreak
From the mischief of those things which He hath created,
From the mischief of the night when it cometh on. (cxiii)
Say: I fly for refuge unto the Lord of men,
The King of men,
The God of men,
From jinn and men. (cxiv)

And always the angel commanded him to be patient and to endure under persecutions, as the prophets had done before him.

Muḥammad, despite everything, was protected by the solidarity of the Hāshimite clan. But the slaves and the weak, without any influential protector, were the target of serious cruelty. They were beaten, and had to lie naked in the full glare of the hot sun on burning flag-stones. The compassionate Abu Bakr one day saw the negro Bilāl, sweltering, dying of thirst and with a large stone on his chest, yet continually repeating his profession of faith: 'One alone! One alone!' He bought him from his master and set him free. Bilāl became the first of the muezzins, and because of his powerful voice was chosen to call the faithful to prayer at Medina. The black fraternities of North Africa have chosen him for their patron.

Menacing threats continued to be made. Muḥammad advised the weakest members to seek refuge in Abyssinia under the protection of the Christian Negus. Sixty or seventy believers, fifteen of whom were women, crossed the Red Sea under the leadership of Ja'far, brother of 'Ali, and were well received. This first 'emigration', like that of 622, bears witness that early Islam not only sympathized with the Christians but was growing away from the tribal conception of ancient Arab civilization towards the conception of a new form of community. The Quraishites felt this, and wished to excommunicate *en masse* all Muslims or, according to some, all the Hāshimite clan. An edict to this effect is said to have been hung on the Ka'bah, but it proved to be impracticable.

It was about this time that Ḥamza, the impetuous giant, and 'Umar ibn al-Khaṭṭāb, the future caliph, were converted.

The Qur'ān throws some light for us on the polemics. The Quraishites clung with great tenacity to their ancestral customs.

The muezzin calls to prayer

('Dost thou forbid us to worship that which our fathers worshipped?' xi, 65, 89.) What reasons had they for following an enlightened impostor or sorcerer who spoke in rhymes and cadences, inspired by devils or demons, or a master-forger who repeated old stories given him by strangers, and who, besides this, performed no miracle in support of his mission? The attack was a subtle one and the Qur'ān repulsed it vigorously.

> Let me alone with him whom I have created,
> On whom I have bestowed abundant riches. . . .
> He said: 'This is no other than magic borrowed from others,
> These are only the words of a man.' (lxxiv, 11–25)
> I swear by that which ye see
> And that which ye see not!
> Truly this is the discourse of an honourable apostle.
> It is not the discourse of a poet. (How little faith ye have!)
> Neither is it the discourse of a soothsayer. (How little are ye admonished!)
> It is a revelation from the Lord of all creatures. (lxix, 38ff.)
>
> The unbelievers say, 'This Qur'ān is no other than a forgery which he hath contrived, and other people have assisted him therein.' [In speaking thus] they utter an unjust thing and a falsehood.
>
> They also say: 'These are fables of the ancients, which he hath caused to be written down; and they are dictated unto him morning and evening. (xxv, 5f.)
>
> Verily We know that they say: 'A certain man teacheth him to compose the Qur'ān.' But the tongue of the person of whom they think is a foreign tongue; whereas this, wherein the Qur'ān is written, is the perspicuous Arabic tongue. (xvi, 105)

External influence in the form of plagiarism and imposture was denied, and the direct inspiration and inimitability of the Qur'ān was confirmed. Men and jinn were challenged to produce a similar discourse, and their failure to do this was the main proof of his divine mission.

The great argument was the example of the ancient prophets. The Qur'ān does not speak in a narrative and historical form, but is dynamic and polemical by nature, embodying one general theme which is constantly repeated: a messenger from God calls men to their duties and to monotheism; his fellow-countrymen do not listen and are punished—as will be the unbelieving Quraishites both in time and at the end of time. Set in spirited sermons, these stories, which do not appear to be drawn from written texts but suggest oral communications ultimately derived from the Bible, the Talmud, the Apocrypha and sometimes purely Arab tradition, have a persuasive force and a striking lyrical quality. Some, for example the story of Abraham's conversion, rise from the sensible to the intelligible, from the relative to the absolute. Others, like the meeting between Moses and the Man with the Fish, al-Khidr, or like the birth of Jesus, the Word of God incarnate in the Virgin, are of great mystical worth. Others again, such as the life of the handsome Joseph, are difficult to improve on for sheer poetry.

> We have destroyed no city but preachers were first sent unto it To admonish the inhabitants thereof; neither did We treat them unjustly. (xxvi, 208f.)

Abraham, Moses, Lot, Jonah, John the Baptist and Jesus have been misunderstood and persecuted, just as were the Arab prophets, Ṣāliḥ by the Thamudites, Hūd by the 'Ādites, and Shu'aib by the Madyanites. Muḥammad had therefore no reason to despair if he did not convert his fellow-countrymen; he is not responsible for the blindness of their hearts. So much the worse for them if they do not understand the inestimable benefit that God is conferring on them, which is to send them a revelation in the Arabic language in order that they might easily come to the Truth. Access to the Truth had hitherto been more difficult for them than for those people who possessed a Book.

> The Scriptures were only sent down unto two peoples before us; and we neglected to peruse them with attention. (vi, 157)

This new Book in a clear Arabic tongue only confirms the previous messages (xlvi, 11):

> This Qur'ān could not have been composed by any except God; but it is a confirmation of that which was revealed before it. (x, 38)

There is only one unique religion of the prophets, and between the prophets no distinctions should be made (Ḥadīth, Bukhāri). The People of the Scriptures approve of the new Prophet, and know that he is truthful. Later, after the misunderstandings, the idea formed that the earlier writings had been corrupted and that the

Qur'ān had come to replace them. For the moment it goes so far as to say:

> If thou art in doubt concerning any part of that which we have sent down unto thee, ask them who read the Scriptures sent down before thee. (x, 94)

The prophets of old, objected the sceptics, performed miracles to prove the authenticity of their mission. Abraham sustained fire without hurt, Moses changed a stick into a serpent, Jesus raised the dead. But you, Muḥammad, who pretend to be visited by an angel, you are not able to show us him, no more than to make a fresh spring gush out or to predict market prices. Muḥammad, however, has never depicted himself as a superman or a miracle-worker.

> Say: I have power neither to procure advantage unto myself, nor to avert mischief from me, but as God pleaseth. If I knew the secrets of God I should surely enjoy abundance of good, neither should evil befall me. Verily I am no other than a denouncer of threats, and a messenger of good tidings unto people who believe. (vii, 188)
>
> Am I other than a man sent as a Messenger? (xvii, 95)

Besides, material miracles would not convince hardened hearts, hearts with a seal over them. The only miracle-proof (*mu'jizah*, peculiar to prophets and distinct from the *karāmah* or charisma of saints) which Muḥammad claims is the inimitable Qur'ān.

THE QUR'ĀN

Muḥammad himself never ceased to marvel at the Qur'ān (the Lection, the Recitation), of which each verse was an *āyah* (sign, proof). He received fragments of it in secondary states which submerged his voluntary and conscious personality, even when they corresponded to its preoccupations. The revelations were sometimes broken off; he waited for them to resolve his difficulties, to give directives to his community from day to day, and to formulate rules when these were felt to be necessary. The revelations grew less abrupt as he grew older and accustomed himself to his role of transmitter. Contact was made and broken more easily; just as in the life of the mystics, after great storms there comes a more serene, more integrated period. But he always made a sharp distinction between what came to him from beyond in these secondary states and what came to him from his own conscious mind, even when it was inspired. The traditionists have preserved a number of ḥadīth in which the Prophet acts, speaks, teaches, commands, makes apologues and sermons, even makes God speak in the first person. But none of them would dream of confusing this with the Qur'ān, and from the style alone all Arabs would at once recognize the difference.

The phenomena which accompanied the revelations were striking. Whenever Muḥammad felt them coming he shivered and trembled and generally covered himself with a shawl or cloak ('O thou who art covered by a cloak', lxxiii, lxxiv), and under this he could be heard blowing, groaning and uttering hoarse cries. He broke out in a sweat and experienced a heaviness of head, which he treated with poultices. Severe muscular tension was also present. After the solemn sermon of the Pilgrimage of Farewell a verse (the last) came down and caused the camel on which he was riding to fall down on its knees. When verse 97 of sura iv was revealed, against those who try to avoid going to the Holy War, the Prophet had his usual secretary, Zaid ibn Thābit, called. A blind man appeared and complained of being criticized for not going, although he could not help it. Muḥammad's thigh was resting on that of Zaid and suddenly weighed so much that the latter became afraid that his would break, while there came down a verse specifying that exception was to be made for the incapacitated. A man had asked 'Umar to show him the Prophet at a moment of revelation. The opportunity presented itself on the road to Mecca. Some one had asked a question about the pilgrimage. Muḥammad was silent. A revelation came to him, 'Umar raised his veil and showed the men the Prophet in a trance. His face was red, he was breathing heavily 'like a calf', then he fell into a torpor from which he emerged saying, 'Where is the man who asked me a question?'

There were various modes of receiving revelations—more or less perfect degrees, it would seem. Sometimes he heard rustlings, bell-like sounds and confused speech, of which he only understood the sense when the noise had stopped. Sometimes the angel appeared in human form, speaking clearly and making himself understood as each word came. Sometimes it seems he had an intuition more direct and intellectual. It must have been a great effort to pass to the state of logical and intelligible speech. The Qur'ān advises the Prophet not to become impatient, not to 'move the tongue to hasten the expression' (lxxv, 16) of a text which God undertook to imprint on his memory.

What became of the fragments received under these conditions? They were secured in the memory of the Prophet and of the faithful, some of whom tried to know by heart as many of them as possible. They were written on skins, palm leaves, pieces of pottery and the shoulder-blades of sheep. At Medina Muḥammad had secretaries who immediately wrote them down.

These fragments were gathered into chapters or suras, which were arranged as nearly as possible in order of length, the shortest, and at the same time the oldest, coming in the main at the end. The long suras themselves are not ordered discourses (except that of Joseph—xii), but collections of fragments, for the most part long, though not necessarily of the same date. At the Prophet's death several Medinans knew the whole by heart. The caliph Abu Bakr, not without hesitation, entrusted its collation to Zaid ibn Thābit. Then the caliph 'Uthmān (644–55) had a vulgate text made on the basis of copies left in charge of Ḥafsah, Muhammad's widow and daughter of 'Umar; and the other copies were burnt.

From childhood Muslims learn verses of the Qur an by heart

The ascension of the Prophet on the mare Buraq.
(*Khamsa of Nizami, Persian ms., B.N.*)*

* The initials *B.N.*, here and elsewhere, are an abbreviation for *Bibliotheque Nationale*, the principal Paris library.

THE YEAR OF GRIEF

'Ye shall surely be proved in your possessions and in your persons', the Qur'ān had proclaimed (iii, 183). After the boycott of the clan of the Hāshimites had been lifted, the Prophet found himself confronted with fresh trials. In 620, 'The Year of Grief', he lost, one after the other, his uncle Abu Ṭālib and his wife Khadījah. Abu Ṭālib had been responsible for his upbringing and had continued to protect him; but on his death-bed he refused to forswear the religion of his forefathers.

Muḥammad tried to proclaim his message in the town of Ṭā'if, but without success. On his return he converted a company of invisible jinn, who had been amazed to hear him chanting the Qur'ān under a palm-tree; and it was by sura lxxii that he learnt this astounding and comforting news; this was to signify that if men did not hear him there were invisible forces which could support him. Back again at Mecca, he had the famous vision known by the name of 'the night journey' (*isrā'*) or 'ascension' (*mi'rāj*); he was carried to Jerusalem on the winged steed Burāq led by Gabriel, and then he ascended, by a ladder of light, from the ruins of the Temple to the foot of the Heavenly Throne. This vision, whose anniversary is celebrated on 27 Rajab each year, and with which is associated the prescribing of the five daily prayers, has given rise to mystic meditations and to a whole literature of fantastic descriptions of Heaven and Hell. As is known, the Abbé Asin Palacios has seen in it a source of Dante's *Divine Comedy*.

'uhammad before the Throne of God.
'ook of the Assumption, in Uighur, Turkish ms., B.N.)

THE HIJRAH

The Hijrah. (Jami' at-Tawarikh, University of Edinburgh, Arabic and Persian mss., no. 20)

Among the Arab tribes the efforts of the Prophet had not been happier than at Ṭā'if. It was from Yathrib that the solution came. The inhabitants of this oasis had been converted by the work of an envoy of Muḥammad's. Some, who had come on pilgrimage to Mecca in 620 and 621, had asked Muḥammad to go to them. In the course of two secret nocturnal meetings they had sworn fidelity and promised to follow his religion and his moral precepts —not to associate any being with God (that is, not to worship idols), not to steal, calumniate or commit adultery, not to kill their children even if they thought that it would not be possible to feed them, and to obey the Prophet in all that was right.

Yathrib was an oasis, where some three thousand people lived, north of Mecca and more inhabitable than it. The population— more peasant and less commercial than the Quraishites—was divided into two hostile tribes, the Aws and the Khazraj. There were also three Jewish groups, the Banu 'n-Nadīr, the Banu Quraiẓah and the Banu Qainūqā'.

Muḥammad sent out about sixty Muslims to Yathrib in small groups. The leaders of Mecca did not seem keen to let him rejoin them. There was even word of a plot to kill him. He hid with Abu Bakr for three days in a cave on Mount Thawr, and with him, on camels brought by accomplices, fled towards Yathrib. There was a price on their heads. But what could happen to two people having God with them? After seven days' travel across a desert of dunes, then of basalt and black lava, they came to the village of Qubā', on the outskirts of the oasis of Yathrib, on Monday 12 First Rabi' (20 September 622). Here 'Ali, who had journeyed on foot, rejoined them. On Friday Muḥammad entered the town which was to become Medina, *madīnat an-nabi*, the city of the Prophet. Under 'Umar about 638 it was decided that this emigration, the Hijrah (or Hegira) should be the point of departure of the Muslim era, but the first day was not 12 First Rabi' but the first day of the first month, Muḥarram, of this year; Friday 1 Muḥarram of the year 1 A.H. (Anno Hegirae) corresponds to 16 July 622 of the Julian calendar.

A new era had in effect just opened. A new theocratic community, outside the traditional tribal organization of Arabia, had just been born. Hostilities had virtually opened against Mecca and the 'holy war'—dangerous alliance of words—was going to be forced on them. In addition the economic situation of the new arrivals in Medina was going to be difficult. They were emigrants, *muhājirūn*, who had sacrificed everything for their faith, leaving their country to follow God according to their conscience. The Medinan Muslims were the Anṣār, the Helpers of the Prophet who owed his security to them. A tie of brotherhood and of community of goods was established between the refugees and some generous hosts. (On this some mystics, like Sidi 'Abu 'l-'Abbās later based themselves in order to advocate a kind of re-distribution of property by almsgiving.) The Medinans were far from being all Muslims; apart from the Jews, who rejected all advances, there remained reserved Arabs little disposed to obey a stranger. Many professed Islam with their lips, but were ready to change according to circumstances, and these formed, round a chief of the Khazraj, 'Abd Allāh ibn Ubayy, who had been disappointed in his ambitions, the dangerous faction of the 'Hypocrites', *munāfiqūn*. Muḥammad needed resilience as much as tenacity. A charter consecrated the newly established community as being 'apart from other men'. All the groups were to lend mutual assistance and together to defend the city. The Jews had freedom of worship, the right to protection, and the obligation to contribute to any war that might come. The Prophet was the final arbiter in each case, and no group was allowed to go out raiding without his permission.

The Emigrants, of whom only a few had been able to take away any money, whose property left behind at Mecca had been confiscated, and who began to be a burden on their hosts (themselves not well off), had recourse, naturally enough, to the traditional practice of hungry bedouin. Small raiding parties were sent out against the Meccan idolaters in the Spring of 623. One of them killed a man during the truce of the sacred months. This caused a scandal even at Medina. Muḥammad disclaimed the chief who had disobeyed his orders, and the Qur'ān, on the other hand, declared that if to fight during the truce of the sacred months was blameworthy, to drive away believers from their home and to hinder them from practising their religion was an even more serious sin. (ii, 214)

THE HOLY WAR

In the Spring of 624 Muḥammad himself set out with three hundred Muslims (seventy of whom were mounted) to intercept the large caravan of the Quraishites which was returning from Syria under the leadership of Abu Sufyān.

Muḥammad took up his position to the south-west of Medina in the valley of Badr, where the track from Medina joins the great caravan route from Damascus to Mecca. Abu Sufyān, warned in time, changed his route and sent for help. A thousand Quraishites, nearly all mounted, set out to destroy the Muslims. The latter had taken up a favourable position near the wells of Badr. Then followed a series of strange combats. There were rhetorical joustings and poetical declamations followed by general mêlée. After a solemn imprecation and exhortations from the Prophet, who promised Paradise in the shadow of the sabres, the Muslims, with the aid of the angels, remained masters of the field. The enemy left much booty, eighty-four prisoners and seventy dead, as against fourteen Muslims killed. A revelation specified that the Prophet had a right to the fifth of the booty, and was to dispose of it to meet the needs of his family, the poor and the army (viii, 42).

The Muslims killed in the holy war, *jihād*, 'in the way of God', bear henceforth the title of martyrs, witnesses, *shuhadā*'.

> Thou shalt in no wise reckon those who have been slain, in the way of God, dead; nay, they are sustained alive with their Lord. (iii, 163)
>
> Verily God hath purchased of the true believers their souls and their substance, promising them the enjoyment of Paradise on condition that they fight in the way of God. (ix, 112)

Henceforth the Qur'ān resounds with exhortations to fight, which do not seem to have been without effect in stimulating the lukewarm. The Prophet was certainly under no illusion as to the disinterestedness of certain people. 'The martyr is he who gives his life for something other than wealth' (ḥadīth). And the Qur'ān :

> Ye seek the goods of this world, and God would give you those of the life to come. (viii, 68)

One ḥadīth makes Muḥammad on his return from an expedition say, 'We return from the lesser holy war (*jihād*) to wage the greater holy war (*mujāhada*)', that is, the spiritual effort of the ascetic or the struggle against oneself. This shows that the Muslim conscience rates deep spiritual values more highly than the holy war.

The Quraishites got ready their revenge and disciplined themselves most strictly, even forbidding mourning for those killed at Badr. They allowed themselves only to write fierce poems, to which the Muslim poets replied. Muḥammad was not fond of poets 'who talk and do nothing', and, above all else, was not desirous of being entangled with those who are inspired by the jinn rather than the angel of Allah; but he made use of them for propaganda purposes. The Arab poet was not only herald, journalist, chronicler, whose sketches preserved and commented on events, he was also a kind of diviner, with habits that were often strange, wearing, for example, only one shoe or brushing

Muḥammad preaching in the mosque of Medina.
(*University of Edinburgh, Arabic ms.*, 161, *f.* 6*b*)

his hair on one side only, in order to mark his inspiration. His abuse was a sort of incantation which by itself created a real fear.

The year went by with some murders not very flattering to either side. The most important action fought was that against the Jews of the Banu Qainūqā‘. The Jews of Medina did not conceal their hostility and had secret intercourse with the Quraishites. They failed to unite, and allowed themselves to be beaten one after the other. A skirmish, in which a Muslim was killed, was made the opportunity for settling the account with the Banu Qainūqā‘. After a fortnight's siege in their *qaṣr* (or fort), they surrendered and were granted their lives, but had to endure exile in the north, giving up their property, their slaves and the debts due to them. Ka‘b ibn al-Ashraf, a rich Jew of Medina, poet and friend of the Quraishites, after a suspicious journey to Mecca, was enticed out of his castle and stabbed to death. Abu Rāfi‘, who was stirring up the northern tribesmen, was killed in his keep near Khaibar. The break with the Jews, who positively refused to recognize in Muḥammad the prophet of the Gentiles proclaimed in the Scriptures (ii, 38; vii, 156; lxi, 6), was of considerable importance in Islam's evolution and in the growth of its consciousness of itself as a distinct religion. The break was emphasized in a spectacular way. Up to that time the Muslims at Medina turned in prayer in the direction of Jerusalem, Bait al-Quds, the House of Holiness. In February 624, a little before the affair with the Qainūqā‘, some believers were about to pray at Qubā' when a messenger, out of breath, came to tell them that a revelation ordered that they should pray henceforth in the direction of the Ka‘bah, the House of God built by Abraham, father of the believers, ancestor of the Arabs through Ishmael, and exponent of the pure religion, the religion of the hanifs. Immediately the faithful changed the *qiblah* and instead of facing north faced south (ii, 119–123, 136; xiv, 40).

For some time, Muḥammad preserved his solidarity with the Christians, even contrasting their example with that of the Jews (v, 85–87; iii, 48; lvii, 27; lxi, 14). The time came, however, when he broke with them also. The Qur'ān always gives to Jesus the titles of Messiah, Word, Spirit coming from God (iv, 169), and even emphasized His role at the end of the world (xliii, 61). But it did not regard him as Saviour, Redeemer and Mediator. It even appears to say that he was not crucified, although this complex passage (iv, 156) also signifies that God has upset the plans of the executioners and 'has raised him to Himself'.* It reproaches the Christians with being divided into numerous sects, with having forgotten a part of what God had taught them (v, 17), with having made of Jesus something other than a messenger and a servant, with having attributed to God a son, and with having introduced

The prayer of the believers facing Mecca

Mary into a trinity, thus making of God a 'third of three' (iv, 169; v, 76f., 116).

Despite this we must not forget the great tolerance and the wise reticences so far removed from fanaticism.

> As to the true believers and the Jews and the Sabians and the Christians and the Zoroastrians and the idolaters, verily God shall judge between them on the day of resurrection, for God is witness of all things. (xxii, 17)
>
> Surely whosoever believe in God and the Last Day and doeth that which is right, though they be Jews or Christians or Sabians,

---

* See Dermenghem, *Vie de Mahomet*, 1950, pp. 116–118.

they shall have their reward with their Lord; there shall come no fear on them, neither shall they be grieved. (ii, 59; v, 73)

If God had pleased, he had surely made you one people; but He hath thought fit to give you different laws, that He might try you in that which He hath given you respectively; therefore strive to excel each other in good works; unto God shall ye all return, and then will He declare unto you that concerning which ye have disagreed. (v, 53)

After having taken their time and raised their courage with various poems, the Quraishites under the command of Abu Sufyān in the Spring of 625 set in motion three thousand warriors; all the able men of the Quraishites, some allied bedouin, and the Aḥābish, sometimes said to be Abyssinian mercenaries, but perhaps only detribalized Arabs. Warned secretly by his uncle al-'Abbās, Muḥammad managed to get together no more than a thousand men and two horses. Contrary to his own judgement the little army, instead of entrenching itself in Medina, moved out and took up a position with its rear on Mount Uḥud. Three hundred Hypocrites deserted at the last moment. Despite the disadvantages, Muḥammad's skilful disposition of the forces nearly gained the victory. But the archers, contrary to orders, left their positions and rushed for the booty. The commander of the cavalry on the Meccan right wing, Khālid ibn al-Walid, was then able to attack the Muslims from the rear. They were thrown into disorder and driven back, some towards Medina, but most towards Mount Uḥud. Muḥammad received a slit lip from a stone, and had a cheek hit by an arrow and two teeth broken. The Quraishites did not know how to exploit their victory. They pillaged, insulted and mutilated the corpses. The beautiful Hind, wife of Abu Sufyān, who had lost her father at Badr at the hands of Ḥamzah, found the latter's body, opened his chest and ate his liver. Abu Sufyān disclaimed these excesses, exchanged from afar invective poems with the Muslims, and marched off, after having given them a rendezvous for the following year. Such, up till now, had been the tradition in the seasonal tribal wars, which were something of the nature of a sport to the Arabs. The vanquished then came to bury their dead at the very place where they had suffered martyrdom. Muḥammad forbade washing their bodies; the witnesses must appear before God covered with their blood and grime.

The Qur'ān draws the morals from the set-back.

It happeneth thus in war; and we cause these days of different success to alternate with each other among men, that God may know those who believe, and may have martyrs from among you. (iii, 134)

Only disobedience had been responsible for the disaster (iii, 145, 153, 159–61).

Muḥammad needed much energy and extraordinary ability to keep the situation at Medina in hand, where his enemies were again raising their heads, and also among the nomadic tribes, where serious incidents occurred. The Jews of Banu 'n-Naḍīr, who had compromised themselves with the Quaraishites and had stupidly been encouraged to resist by the Hypocrites, had to go into exile, taking with them only those of their belongings which could be loaded on to six hundred camels.

Then, in high summer, Muḥammad went to punish some bedouin who had massacred a group of Muslims. On this occasion the Prayer of Danger was instituted (iv, 103); each group of warriors prayed in turn in the direction of Mecca, making only one prostration, while the others faced the enemy.

In the following year, March 627, four thousand men, Quraishites and bedouin from Nejd, set out against Medina, where Abu Sufyān was assured of spies among the Hypocrites and the remaining Jews, the Banu Quraiẓah. On this occasion also the Muslims were saved from disaster by the intelligence of their leader and the incredible wavering of their enemies. On the advice of Salmān the Persian, a huge ditch was dug round the town and guarded by archers. Neither the Hypocrites nor the Jews moved. Disconcerted by an altogether new stratagem, the attackers were content with setting up camp some distance from the trench or ditch. Worked upon by propaganda the bedouin fled. The angels and a tornado succeeded in upsetting the Quraishites, who also departed (xxxiii, 9). The three thousand mobilized Muslims easily crushed the Banu Quraiẓah (xxxiii, 26f.), who were brutally massacred or reduced to slavery. The Hypocrites understood, and it was the end of all opposition at Medina.

The Muslims now had the initiative. In April 628 Muḥammad set out with fifteen hundred believers to make the Pilgrimage. They halted at Ḥudaibiya, since the Quraishites had occupied the pass giving entry to the sacred territory. Parleys took place. Muḥammad gave in, and had to throw all his authority into the balance to pacify his men. An agreement was signed: the Muslims were to return home now and to come back the following year and only for the '*umrah*, a devout visit or minor pilgrimage; and they undertook not to accept converted deserters. Muḥammad's political good sense helped him to understand the value of a moderation which would allow him to pick without difficulty the fruit soon to become ripe.

> Verily We have granted thee a manifest victory, that God may forgive thee thy preceding and thy subsequent sin, and may complete His favour on thee. (xlviii, 1f.)

Once more the Prophet was to turn the belligerent fire of his people and their greed for booty against the Jews. There were no longer any at Medina, but they possessed the rich oasis of Khaibar, a hundred miles to the north, which had welcomed a part of the Medinan refugees and had become a centre of hostile propaganda on the route to Syria. The battle was violent; the Muslims had to wipe out by assault many small forts and the chief keep. They gained considerable booty. The defeated survivors were allowed to remain as tenants. Muḥammad, it is said, was almost poisoned by a woman captive. He took another, the beautiful Ṣafīyah, to be his wife.

Muhammad and his Companions: his two grandsons, the first four caliphs, the negro muezzin Bilal, etc., in the mosque at Medina. (*17th century Indo-Persian miniature. Carfax Collection. From Sir Thomas Arnold*)

THE HAREM

His harem was now that of a great chieftain, and the rooms of his wives, built around the courtyard of the mosque, had increased in number. Before leaving Mecca he had married the devout Ṣawḍah, the elderly widow of an emigrant to Abyssinia, and had become engaged to the very young and very pretty 'Ā'ishah, the daughter of Abu Bakr, whom he married at Medina. They were joined by Ḥafṣah, daughter of 'Umar, and then, not without some hesitation, the beautiful Zainab, wife of his adopted son Zaid, whom the latter had divorced. A revelation (xxxiii, 37) made it quite clear that Muḥammad was not the father of any man (what ratified the exclusive character of his prophetic mission was his renunciation of having a successor of his own blood), and that God had decreed this marriage to make it clear that a man has the right to marry a woman divorced by his adopted son. On another occasion the jealous 'Ā'ishah, who had a well-oiled tongue, is supposed to have said to her husband, according to the ḥadīth, 'It seems that God is hastening to satisfy your desires'. After the battle of Uḥud he married Umm Salamah, widow of another emigrant to Abyssinia, then the Jewesses Raihānah and Ṣafīyah, after the expeditions against Banu Quraiẓah and Khaibar, then Umm Ḥabībah, daughter of the pagan leader Abu Sufyān and widow of another emigrant to Abyssinia, a Christian ḥanīf, then Maimūnah, sister-in-law of his uncle al-'Abbās and aunt of Khālid ibn al-Walīd, the greatest general of the Quraish.

He also had two or three concubines, one of whom was Maria the Copt, sent to him by the governor of Egypt. This Maria bore him a male child, Ibrāhim, who died at an early age. On that day an eclipse of the sun took place, and there were people who liked to think it was an omen. But Muḥammad, who knew himself and did not want to be more than a man, had the nobility of mind to announce that 'the stars never veil themselves for the death of any creature'.

These marriages of love or of expediency had important consequences. The intrigues of the harem reflected political intrigues and had repercussions in history.

'Ali had married Fāṭimah, Muḥammad's daughter, shortly after the battle of Badr. Two children were born of the union, Ḥasan and Ḥusain, the sole descendants of the Prophet who were to produce a continuing line (whose members, known as *shurafā'*, plural of *sharīf*, are numerous today in both east and west). If one goes by blood-relationship, the position of 'Ali, Fātimah and their children was a strong one. Later, the legitimist Shi'ites claimed the temporal and spiritual heritage of the Prophet for the line of *imāms* issuing from 'Ali, who, they thought, passed from one to another a spiritual, almost divine, spark. The Shi'ites accuse the orthodox Sunnites of having suppressed the Qur'ānic verses and ḥadīth favourable to 'Ali's claims. They assert that Muḥammad had designated him for his successor at Ghadīr on his way back from the Pilgrimage of Farewell. Their miniatures like to represent the touching scene of the *mubāhalah*, of the Five in the Cloak, when Muḥammad, in debate with the Christians from Najrān, offered himself for a trial by ordeal along with those he held most dear,

The Mubahala. Proposing to the Christians of Najran a trial by ordeal on the question of Jesus, Muhammad offers as pledges himself, his daughter Fatima, his son-in-law 'Ali and his two grandsons. (17th century copy of a 14th century miniature. B.N.)

'Ali, Fātimah, Ḥasan and Ḥusain. The deputation from Najrān shrank from the trial and signed a treaty in which they received very liberal terms, while the decision on the christological question was deferred to the end of time.

To this the Sunnites, while respecting the *shurafā'* (true or even false) reply by the ḥadīth, 'A single verse from the Book of God is more valuable than Muḥammad and all his family', which is, it seems, more genuinely in the spirit of fiercely transcendentalist Islam.

The other sons-in-law of the Prophet were Abu 'l-'Ās, who remained at Mecca, and 'Uthmān, who married successively Ruqaiyah and Umm Kulthūm. But they had no descendants; their wives died young, and the importance of 'Uthmān only became apparent later. To the 'Ali-Fātimah *ménage* was opposed the harem party, although the harem itself was much divided. The favourite wife was always 'Ā'ishah. But the beautiful Zainab was for a long time loved and influential. 'Ā'isha, the daughter of Abu Bakr, was in alliance with Hafṣah, the daughter of 'Umar, and these two men were second to none in political sagacity and energy. Ṣawḍah and Ṣafīyah kept themselves in the background but supported 'Ā'ishah and Ḥafṣah. Umm Salamah, Zainab and the other wives formed the second party, which represented in a sense the ancient Meccan aristocracy in opposition to the new men.

The sīrah conscientiously relates spicy disputes between the three groups. These disputes almost caused a tragedy over the affair of 'Ā'ishah's necklace. The Prophet generally took one of his wives with him when he went on campaign. After the expedition against the Banu Mustalīq, 'Ā'ishah, looking for a necklace which she had lost, got left behind, and next day was brought into the camp by a young bedouin. Tongues wagged, and lampoons were composed. The opposition raised its head. 'Ā'ishah wept. 'Ali wanted to see her divorced. Muḥammad in consternation waited for more than a month for a revelation, and eventually it came suddenly, justifying the accused and ordering the slanderers to be punished (xxiv, 11).

On another occasion, at the end of a dispute between Hafsah and Maria the Copt, Muḥammad almost divorced all his wives. 'Umar, who held the ideas of the old Quraishites about how to treat women, reprimanded his daughter, but made an effort to settle the matter. The Prophet slept alone on his terrace for a month.

The Qur'ān declared that he would be able to find other, and better, wives. The harem gave in. But Muḥammad undertook not to marry any other wives (at that time he had nine). As 'Mothers of the Faithful' his wives were not allowed to remarry after his death; they had to go veiled and were not allowed to speak to other men except from behind a curtain (lxvi, 1–5; xxxiii, 51–53). Certainly the attitude of the Prophet as regards women has weighed heavily on Muslim civilization, for the examples and principles were forcibly warped by the natural tendency of men to seek their own advantage. He certainly improved woman's lot in the Arabia of his day. He prohibited infanticide and the prostitution of slave-women. He established the rights of women to inherit (a half-share). He proclaimed that 'Paradise is at a mother's knees', that married couples have reciprocal duties and rights, and that women ought to be educated. He limited the number of wives a man may lawfully have to four. He did not set himself up as a model. As it was, he hardly surprised his contemporaries; on the contrary they were inclined to admire his amatory prowess, and were accustomed, like the contemporaries of Solomon, to measure the power of a ruler by the number of his wives. Polygamy was only permitted if one was capable of being perfectly fair to all. Concubines could only be obtained from the holy war, not from the purchase of slaves. Daughters could not be married without their own consent, and this ought to have done away with the right of *jabr* (arranging marriages for minors). As for unilateral divorce which, more than the now rapidly disappearing polygamy, is the curse of Muslim family life, it is condemned in the famous but little observed ḥadīth, 'There is nothing created that God likes better than the freeing of slaves, and nothing that He hates more than divorce'.

Instead of taking advantage of these rules to move in a liberal and progressive direction, jurisprudence and morals have on the contrary made them more rigid. If the ulema of today wanted, as Muḥammad 'Abduh and Rashīd Riḍā suggested, to employ *ijtihād* (individual interpretation, as opposed to *taqlid*, the formal acceptance of authority), they could, we see, find many arguments in the Qur'ān and the hadīth.

Muhammad and 'Ali overturn the idols in the Ka'bah after the conquest of Mecca (Hist. de Mirkhond, Luzac ms., B.N.)

THE CAPTURE OF MECCA, VICTORY AND DEATH

Victory was drawing near. The Arabian peninsula was about to be purged of idolatry. Mecca, an ungrateful homeland, but one always dear to him, was about to fall like a ripe fruit, thanks to a wisdom and a daring moderation which cannot but be admired. Victory came under conditions such as make this historic event one of the kind which bring honour to the human race. At Ḥudaibiya Muḥammad had shown that he could control his own impatience and that of his followers. Now he was about to bring off the 'resounding victory' promised by revelation. The bloody defeat suffered at Mu'tah in the north by his adopted son Zaid at the hands of the Ghassānids (Christian Arab vassals of the Byzantines) had not lowered his prestige. Already Khālid ibn al-Walīd, the excellent general who saved the remnant of the army at Mu'tah, feeling that the wind was changing, had become a Muslim. He was followed by important Quraishites, 'Amr ibn al-'Ās, the future conqueror of Egypt, and al-'Abbās, Muḥammad's uncle and the ancestor of the future dynasty of caliphs in Baghdad. In accordance with the stipulations of the truce Muhammad made his 'pious visit' to Mecca, which was vacated for three days by most of its inhabitants to allow the Muslims to perform the rites of the pilgrimage (March 629, year VII of the Hijrah). Here once again Muḥammad resisted the temptation to stay on by force. Abu Sufyān, who in spite of himself had become Muḥammad's father-in-law, came to Medina to see his daughter, Umm Ḥabībah, and to spy out the land. After that, in Ramaḍān VIII (January 630), ten thousand armed Muslims set out for the holy city. Abu Sufyān then allowed himself to be taken by a patrol and drew up the terms of capitulation after he too had abjured idolatry. Almost without striking a blow the Prophet entered Mecca and overturned the idols in the Ka'bah ('Truth has come, error is scattered'), grasped the golden ring on the gate of the temple with his hand, and proclaimed an amnesty from which only four pagans were excluded. Then he went to pray at the tomb of Khadījah, first of the faithful and first confidante of his great plan.

There was a dangerous battle at Ḥunain against the Hawāzin encamped to the south of Mecca near Tā'if (end of January 630). The Medinans, disturbed at the policy of 'reconciling the hearts', were sometimes silent. The bedouin showed scant enthusiasm for becoming truly converted (ix, 98–100). There was a difficult expedition of doubtful success to Tabuk near the Byzantine frontier. Yet none of this shook the authority of Muḥammad nor prevented him sending parties in several directions to destroy idols or from signing pacts with the tribes, like that with the Christians of Najrān in the south and of Aila in the north (granting liberty of conscience and protection in return for the payment of a poll-tax).

At the pilgrimage of the year IX (631), presided over by Abu Bakr, 'Ali had to proceed from Medina to Mecca by forced marches to read a revelation (ix, 3–5) just received by Muḥammad which made idolatry illegal. In the following year Muḥammad himself came with ninety thousand pilgrims to perform rites which now became definitively fixed in Islam: the taking of the simple pilgrim dress of the *iḥrām* and the entry into the state of taboo; the seven circumambulations, at two different paces, round the Ka'bah of Abraham; the veneration of the Black Stone; the running between the hills of al-Ṣafā and al-Marwah in memory of Hagar and Ishmael; the standing at the foot of Mount 'Arafāt; the sermon (on the 9th) on Mount 'Arafāt, where Adam and Eve had been; the rapid descent to Muzdalifa towards nightfall; the stoning of the three pillars called demons; the sacrifices of sheep and camels at Minā

The Pilgrims on Mount 'Arafat on the day before the great sacrifice.
(*La vie de Mahomet, by E. Dinet and Sliman ben Ibrahim, Piazza*, 1918)

E. DINET

(on the 10th); the ending of the taboo by the cutting of the hair and the nails; and another visit to the holy places.

This was the Pilgrimage of Farewell. Muḥammad preached himself on Mount 'Arafāt. He exhorted the Arabs to remain united in Islam after his death, proclaimed the reciprocal rights and duties of married couples, the abolition of usury and the blood-feud, and the fixing of the year at twelve lunar months without solar correction, asked the crowd twice, 'Have I accomplished my mission?' and received the last *āya* (verse) revealed, 'Today I have made perfect your religion; I have fulfilled My grace upon you and I am pleased that your faith should be Islam' (v, 5).

On returning to Medina he fell ill, and his death took place on Monday, 13 First Rabi' of the year XI (8 June, 632).

Perhaps it is fitting to set down here the impartial and balanced judgement of Régis Blachère, a recent biographer of the Prophet, whose aim has simply been to make an 'attempt at a critical biography of the founder of Islam' without concession to either romance or hagiography. 'Neither indifference, nor wounds to his self-respect, nor wrong done to his material interests, nor intrigues nor threats, nor, above all, the many offers of compromise made by the pagans, were able to deflect him from his mission. In the gravest hours—the Qur'ān bears witness—he could retain his balanced judgement, revive the courage of his followers, and close his eyes to slight faults in order the better to destroy treason. As a true leader of men, he knew how to choose his advisers,

The mosque of Medina which contains the tomb of the Prophet. (18th century miniature)

turning to account the faithfulness of 'Ali, the moderation of Abu Bakr, the energy of 'Umar and the resilience of 'Uthmān. He had no illusions about men, and never failed to remind them of their duty and their vocation. Better than anyone, too, he knew the faults and virtues of the people among whom he was born. This inspired man, who never for a day had thought of succeeding without God's help, yet knew how to look into the future and to measure the strength and weakness of his adversary. Whatever may be said of him he was a good and generous man. At the taking of Mecca his clemency was more than a politic act. Hagiography, as always, has done a bad turn to its hero. With its naïveté, its miracles to order and its insipidity, it is forced, in order to satisfy popular needs, to raise to the role of miracle-worker one who, the Qur'ān never ceased to repeat, was a mortal like all other men. If, at his last hour, Muḥammad had asked himself about the success of his mission, he could have passed to his rest in the serenity of knowing that he had fulfilled his task.'*

* Régis Blachère, *Le probleme de Mahomet*, 1952, p. 129.

THE CIVIL WARS AND THE CONQUESTS

Muḥammad's death was followed by great confusion. The Hāshimites were left to deal with his corpse, and Abu Bakr and 'Umar had not even time to be present at his funeral. The former vigorously proclaimed the continuity of Islam. 'If you worship Muḥammad, know that he is dead; but if you worship God, know that God is living.' The Anṣār had met together, and seemed determined to give the power to a Medinan. The two fathers-in-law of the Prophet went in company to the assembly, and in two able speeches succeeded in keeping 'Ali as well as the Anṣār from the caliphate. Abu Bakr was elected. During his two years of reign he suppressed tribal revolts and stabilized the situation in the peninsula. He died in 634 after appointing 'Umar as his successor. The latter zealously pursued the conquests, died in 644 when he was murdered by a Persian Christian, and was succeeded by 'Uthmān. The latter had much less drive, and under him divisions set in to a dangerous extent. He was assassinated in 656. 'Ali was then elected, but his five years of caliphate were little more than a perpetual battle against the various parties: at the battle of the Camel he took his old enemy 'Ā'isha prisoner and generously freed her; the battle of Ṣiffīn in 657 against the armies of Mu'āwiyah the Umayyad, the son of Abu Sufyān and governor of Syria, had the result that 'Ali, who had accepted an arbitration to stop the fratricidal war, was odiously duped and had his claims set aside; the battle of Nahrawān (658) was against the Khārijites or secessionists, who accused him of having been a traitor by allowing his right to succeed to be called in question (at the arbitration), and who were responsible for his assassination in 661. Mu'āwiyah was then proclaimed caliph, and the caliphate properly so called became a hereditary monarchy for the benefit of the Umayyad dynasty of Damascus. These were replaced by the

Hāshimite 'Abbāsids of Baghdad (750–1258), who, though descendants of al-'Abbās, uncle of the Prophet, did not show themselves to be less severe towards his direct descendants, the 'Alids. The tragedy of Kerbela (680), when 'Ali's son Ḥusain and all his family were massacred by the army of Yazīd, son and successor of Mu'āwiyah, is commemorated among the Shi'ites by processions of flagellants and 'passion-plays'.

These unhappy divisions among the Companions of the Prophet did not stop the lightning progress of the Muslim armies. They were generally well-received by the populations of the Sassanian, Byzantine and Visigothic empires, which collapsed with startling rapidity: the Byzantines were defeated at the Yarmuk in 636, the Persians at al-Qādisiyah in 637 and at Nahāwand in 642; Alexandria was taken in 642, Kairouan in 670, Toledo in 712, Herat in 661, Transoxiana in 711. It took the victory of Charles Martel in 732 to halt them at Poitiers, while thanks to the use of Greek fire the Byzantines resisted successfully in 678 and 717. In 756, as Baghdad was becoming the capital of the 'Abbāsids in the east, an Umayyad caliphate was being set up at Cordova.

This is not the place to trace the history of the Muslim countries throughout thirteen centuries, but it is necessary to give some idea of the various aspects of the Islamic tradition and of its development.

'Ali and his two sons.
(Modern popular picture, Algeria)

The Shahadah. La ilah illa 'llah, Muhammad rasul Allah; there is no god but God, and Muhammad is the Messenger of God. Above: Huwa 'llah; it is He, God!

THE FIVE PILLARS

As we have seen in describing the life of the Prophet, the fundamental principles of his religion at its origin were clear and perfectly simple. The Five Pillars of Islam are: (1) the profession of faith, *tashahhud*, according to the well-known formula, the *shahādah*: 'There is no god but God, and Muḥammad is the Messenger of God'; (2) the canonical prayer or worship, *ṣalāt*, five times a day at fixed hours, preceded by ablutions, with attitudes and prostrations strictly ordered, and with slight variants according to the different legal rites (this is distinct from supererogatory prayer, *nāfilah*, from nocturnal prayer, *tahajjud*, from the prayer of asking, *du'ā'*, and from the prayer for the dead, *ṣalāt al-janāzah*; (3) the fast, *ṣawm*, for twenty-nine or thirty days in the month of Ramaḍān, fixed by the visual observation of the crescent moon, with abstinence by day from all eating, drinking, smoking and sexual excitement; (4) the legal tithe, *zakāt*, as distinguished from the voluntary charitable alms, *ṣadaqah*, and the customary alms at the breaking of the fast; (5) the pilgrimage, *ḥajj*, to Mecca (the essential rites of which we have described) and to Medina, where the Prophet's tomb is venerated—it was violated by the Wahhābis in 1806, but they have not dared to stop the visits to it.

It would be interesting to see how the Five Pillars work out in practice in various countries. The faith is rigorous and absolute, so much so that one has been able to specify each of the three religions of Abraham by one of the three theological virtues, faith especially characterizing Islam, hope Judaism, and charity Christianity. Prayer is not perhaps carried out rigorously everywhere five times a day. Contrary to what one might believe, the practice is tending to grow. The *zakāt* is difficult to single out, since a variety of taxes are added to it or replace it. The voluntary alms are given very generously, and include hospitality, *diyāfah*, and the *ḥubus* or *awqāf* (or *wuqūf*), pious foundations and trusts; some are public and have performed many social services; others are private and are often a method of avoiding the rules of inheritance. The fast is strictly observed nearly everywhere. Individuals away from a Muslim environment sometimes dispense with it, though not without some uneasiness of conscience, when they find it too difficult to carry out, for it presupposes the complete modification of a form of communal life. As for the pilgrimage, it makes concrete in a formal way the solidarity of the *ummah*, the international religious community.

The pilgrims throw seven stones at the great satan of Mina, a pillar of masonry. (Photograph by Jean Roman)

The prayer of the North African pilgrims on the boat conveying them to Jeddah. (*Jean Roman: 'Le Pelerinage aux Lieux Saints de l'Islam', Baconnier, Algiers*)

The Ka'bah. Fervent hands are stretched up to the raised door of the house of Allah. (Jean Roman; 'Le Pelerinage . . .')

'We appointed the holy house to be a place of resort for mankind and a place of security; and said, Take the station of Abraham for a place of prayer; and We covenanted with Abraham and Ishmael that they should cleanse My house for those who should compass it. (*Qur'an*, ii, 119) (*Jean Roman*, 'Le Pelerinage . . .')

It is the dream of the religious life of the believer, and its consecration. For it considerable sacrifices are made, although it is not strictly obligatory unless it can be accomplished without too much danger and difficulty.

The content of faith, *imān*, is very simple.

> O true believers, believe in God and His messenger and the Book which He hath caused to come down unto His messenger, and the Scriptures which He hath formerly sent down; whosoever believeth not in God and His angels and His scriptures and His messengers and the Last Day, he surely erreth in a wide mistake. (iv, 135; cf. ii, 172, 285)

Allah is the unique God, without partner, incomparable, the only necessary Being, absolute, self-subsisting, self-sufficient, (the Sufis later say, 'the only absolute Reality'), 'the greatest' compared with others, the Highest, the Sublime, the Magnificent, the Praiseworthy, the Holy, the Living, the Eternal, the Creator, the Almighty, the Judge, the Benefactor, the Clement, the Pitiful, the Guardian, the Protector, the Just, the Gentle, the Compassionate, the First and the Last, the Apparent and the Hidden, the One by whom all live and to whom all return. He is transcendent, and the tenacity of the theologians is continually erecting barriers between the incommensurable Being and the world. But He is none the less immanent, as some of His names indicate and as the mystics insist: 'nearer to you than your jugular vein' (l, 15), the only one to whom the name *al-Ḥaqq*, the Truth, can adequately be given. There is no room for an opposition of apophatic and cataphatic theology, nor of exoteric and esoteric doctrines, for in Islam these complement each other harmoniously. The *tawḥid* is the theology of the belief in the one, unique God; it is also, for the mystics, the science of unification.

As for these Beautiful Names and Attributes, there were debates whether they belonged to the divine essence or not. The Mu'tazilites with their rationalistic tendencies were believers in freedom of the will, and held that there is an absolute good and an absolute evil, and that God is of necessity good and just, not an arbitrary despot. To avoid anthropomorphism and what they judged to be a disguised polytheism they rejected the attributes. They declared that the Divine Essence was alone eternal and that the Qur'ān was God's created word, whereas the great majority of the Sunnites believe that the attributes are co-eternal and the Qur'ān uncreated. This amounts perhaps to what Christians understand by the Word.

Likewise, the orthodox theologians, despite quite a number of exceptions, starting from the fact that God knows, originates and creates everything, generally believe in predestination, *qadar*, and deny man's freedom although, without understanding it, they admit his responsibility. Moreover, Qur'ān and Ḥadīth contain texts supporting both views. The Qur'ān frequently declares that God guides as He wills, gives His grace to whom he wills, and misleads those whom He wills. Régis Blachère (*op. cit.*, pp. 75–78) has shown that several of these passages seem especially to correspond to the agonies of the Prophet and the first Muslims confronted by what seemed to them the incomprehensible obstinacy of the polytheists (vi, 39, 125; x, 75; xvi, 39, 95; xvii, 47f.). Goldziher points out that God does not lead men into error, but allows them to err, threatening not to save the obstinate ones from their blindness. Other passages describe how men's destinies are eternally fixed on the well-guarded Tablet, and how God causes men to live, to die and to rise again as He wills, and how all things are in His hands (iii, 139; ix, 51; xxxv, 25; xxxvi, 11; lxxx, 18–22). This idea is to be found in many of the religions which believe in God's omnipotence and providence. The verse taken as a basis of the view, 'it is God who hath created you and what ye do' (xxxvii, 94), can signify not that man is irrelevant to his acts since God exercises compulsive power over them, but that all things, all substance and all energy coming as they do from God the creator, the acts of created beings could obviously not exist without Him. The Sufis set out from here to assert not determination but adhesion, a transforming union; human beings have no other existence than that which they gain from participation in real divine Existence. 'Neither didst thou shoot the arrow .... but God shot it' (viii, 17).

Other verses, however, speak as though man were free; God does no wrong to anyone (xviii, 28; xxxviii, 25; iv, 52; xli, 16). And the following verses state magnificently the place and responsibility of man in the universe:

> When thy Lord drew forth their posterity from the lions of the sons of Adam, and took them to witness against themselves, saying, Am I not your Lord? they answered, Yea, we do bear witness. We did this lest ye should say at the day of resurrection, We knew not of this matter. (vii, 171)

We proposed faith unto the heavens and the earth and the mountains; and they refused to undertake the same, and were afraid thereof; but man undertook it; verily he has become unjust and foolish. (xxxiii, 72)

The social consequences of the current interpretation of the *maktūb* or 'what is written' could be serious. Obviously in practice men do not act, or refuse to act, as if all were hopeless. But instead of being only a courageous attitude, a wise and stoic resignation in the face of the inevitable—whether the inevitable be thought of as that which does not depend on us, with Epictetus, or as the will of God, with religious men—the *maktūb* could easily become a lazy attitude of indifference and drift, whereas it ought to be an intelligent remedy against worry, and an encouragement to fruitful patience. When a bedouin asked if it was necessary to secure his camel, the Prophet replied, 'Secure thy camel, and trust in God'. He also gave the exhortation, 'Act, the task will be made easy for you', which is the equivalent of 'God helps him who helps himself'.

The *jihād* or holy war is not included in the Five Pillars. It was only an occasional communal obligation, and it is only too evident that one cannot discuss the 'holiness' of its character. Temporal powers naturally tend to make use of it; but modern lawyers have expressed the opinion that the only holy wars were those of the Prophet. It is equally wrong to suppose that Islam advanced by the sword. 'Let there be no constraint in religion; now is truth manifestly distinguished from error' (ii, 257). The warlike exhortations of the Qur'ān applied to specific contemporary circumstances and varied with them. The Islamic empire admitted into its fold the Christian and Jewish 'People of the Book' (and even the Mazdeans or Zoroastrians, and indeed later the Hindus, since they too had sacred books); they had their own statute (giving internal autonomy), were exempt from military service, and paid, not the *zakāt* which was reserved for converts to Islam, but the poll-tax (*jizyah*) and the land-tax (*kharāj*). In India (as in black Africa today) conversions were brought about more by the influence of the brotherhoods and the santons (whom some miniatures depict fraternizing with the yogis) than by arms. In the Muslim conscience still, though somewhat repressed today, is the ideal of transforming the non-Muslim world into *dār al-Islām*, that is, into territory which is either Muslim or is tributary to a Muslim ruler.

As is commonly observed in sociology, it is not always the most formally prescribed customs which are carried out most strictly. A Muslim who has given up prayer will refuse with horror to eat pork, and will regard circumcision as the essential external element in belonging to Islam. Circumcision is only a sunna (custom) mentioned in the Ḥadīth but not in the Qur'ān. Alimentary rules, less numerous than in the Bible, deal with pork and the blood of animals (v, 4); animals must be slaughtered by having their throats cut, while the formula must be pronounced, '*Bismillāh; Allāhu akbar*' (In the name of God; God is greatest). It is forbidden to kill uselessly and to cause animals suffering. As to wine and alcoholic drinks, the prohibition (not always strictly observed, but all the same curbing much alcoholism among the masses) proceeds in stages: warnings against the dangers of wine and gaming, prohibition against prayer when in a state of drunkenness, precise details that strong drink is more of a handicap than an advantage. Then, after a scandal caused by Ḥamzah at the marriage of 'Ali, proof that wine and games of chance were means used by Satan to produce discord; then a formal reprobation against wine, gaming and sacrifices to idols (ii, 216; iv, 46; v, 92).

The prohibitions against the cult of idols (vi, 74; xiv, 38; etc.) have resulted in raising the whole question of images, and this has left a peculiar stamp on Muslim art. Points of view differ according to period and country. The prohibition—if prohibition there is—has been no better observed than that of wine. The countless celebrated Persian miniatures are not the only ones. But the development of sculpture and of painting properly speaking, as we have known it in Europe since the fifteenth century, has been hindered. On the other hand decoration, arabesque in chiselled work or in paint, abstract art, have been popular, and have been brought to a high degree of perfection. The underlying idea is that man must avoid competing presumptuously against the divine Creator. At the Last Judgement God will challenge the artists to make their works live, and they will be embarrassed not to be able to perform this. Sculpture, above all, is generally condemned, since it produces a shadow. The portrayal of the Prophet is also condemned, but, as can be seen from the illustrations in this book, there are exceptions; besides in most cases the precaution is taken to show his face veiled or without features. If the human face and the realistic animal form is set aside, the artists are left to make objects resembling flowers, said Ibn 'Abbās to one of them.

بسم الله الرحمن الرحيم
ابو بكر
عمر
عثمان
علي
عن علي رضي الله تعالى عنه
كان اذا وصف النبي صلى الله عليه وسلم قال
لم يكن بالطويل الممغط ولا بالقصير المتردد كان ربعة
من القوم ولم يكن بالجعد القطط ولا بالسبط كان
جعدا رجلا ولم يكن بالمطهم ولا بالمكلثم وكان في الوجه
تدوير ابيض مشرب ادعج العينين اهدب الاشفار
جليل المشاش والكتد اجرد ذو مسربة شثن الكفين
والقدمين اذا مشى يتقلع كانما يمشي في صبب
واذا التفت التفت معا
وما ارسلناك الا رحمة للعالمين
بين كتفيه خاتم النبوة وهو خاتم النبيين اجود الناس صدرا واصدقهم
لهجة والينهم عريكة واكرمهم عشيرة من رآه بديهة هابه
ومن خالطه معرفة احبه يقول ناعته لم ار قبله ولا بعده مثله صلى الله عليه وسلم
اللهم صل وسلم على نبي الرحمة وشفيع الامة محمد واله وصحبه اجمعين الطاهرين
كتبه الحاج احمد كامل المعروف رئيس الخطاطين غفر الله ذنوبه امين
١٣٥٧

If Muslim art has not produced a Michaelangelo or a Rembrandt, one can appreciate that it has produced the mosques of Cordova, Fez, Kairouan, Cairo, the Alhambra, the Taj Mahal and other masterpieces of architecture and decorative art from Spain to the Indies. Uniformity is not desirable, and it is a good thing that each one follows his own bent.

The other prescriptions of canon law which are important, since they show the various sides and the principal nuances of Islamic tradition, are those dealing with personal status, such as marriage or divorce of which we have already spoken, and those of public law.

The almost exclusive attention paid by scholars to canonical jurisprudence (*fiqh*), to the detriment of the disciplines of literature and philosophy, can even be considered as one of the chief aspects of the decadence which showed itself wholesale towards the thirteenth century.

Portrait of the Prophet in writing
(text in the circle and rectangle)
Above: Bismillah ar-rahman ar-rahim
(In the name of God, the Merciful, the Compassionate)
In the four corners the names of the first four caliphs,
Abu Bakr, 'Umar, 'Uthman, 'Ali
Below, a verse of the Qur'an:
'We have not sent thee save as a mercy for the worlds'
Such charts are found today in all the old families of Algiers.

RITES AND SECTS

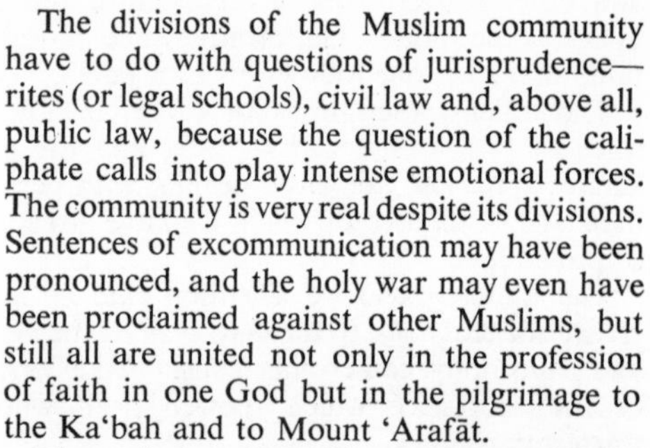

The divisions of the Muslim community have to do with questions of jurisprudence—rites (or legal schools), civil law and, above all, public law, because the question of the caliphate calls into play intense emotional forces. The community is very real despite its divisions. Sentences of excommunication may have been pronounced, and the holy war may even have been proclaimed against other Muslims, but still all are united not only in the profession of faith in one God but in the pilgrimage to the Ka‘bah and to Mount ‘Arafāt.

The majority of Muslims are Sunnis, claiming that they follow the *sunnah*, the habitual usage of the Prophet, of his Companions, of the first four 'rightly-guided' caliphs, and of the immediate Successors. To the Qur'ān and the sunnah may be added to make the rules more specific the *ijmā‘* or consensus of the scholars, the *ra'y* or personal interpretation of a sound scholar, *qiyās* or analogical reasoning, and *istiḥsān* or *istislāh* the consideration of public welfare.

The Sunnis are divided into four rites or legal schools (*madhāhib*, sing. *madhhab*), which only differ in the relative importance which they attach to each of these roots (*ijmā‘*, etc.), and in some details of ritual and of law. The Ḥanbalite and Mālikite rites are the strictest. The first, formerly common in Syria and Iraq, is today confined to central Arabia; the second holds almost undisputed sway in North Africa and the Sudan. The Ḥanafite rite, which expanded after the Ottomans adopted it, predominates in Turkey, India and China, the Shāfi‘ite rite in southern Arabia, in eastern and southern Africa, in Indonesia and in Egypt.

Minaret of the mosque Al-Azhar, Cairo.

It is permissible to change from one rite to another, and all are taught at Al-Azhar. Some scholars have succeeded in making the law flexible by drawing on whichever rite gave the principle most in accordance with modern ideas.

On the other hand there is a complete cleavage between the orthodox and the two bodies of schismatics founded on two directly opposed attitudes, the Shī'ites and the Khārijites, whose origins we have described.

As legitimists, the Shī'ites or 'partisans' of the family of the Prophet detest the first three caliphs, especially 'Umar, who in their eyes usurped the rights of 'Ali. The more moderate or Twelvers agree in applying to 'Ali and his eleven direct successors the principle of hereditary succession to spiritual and temporal powers, together with infallibility and sinlessness. The twelfth and last imām disappeared, remains in hiding, and will return at the Last Day. To know the imām of the age or to have faith in the hidden imām assures a man of salvation. The Shī'ites in consequence reject the evolutionary principle of *ijmā'* or consensus accepted by the Sunnis. But they attach still more authority than the latter to the scholars (*mujtahids*) who, in the name of the hidden imām, practise *ijtihād* or individual interpretation. This has been given up by the Sunnis since the establishment of the four rites, but in recent days the followers of Muḥammad 'Abduh and Rashīd Riḍā have tried to revive it. Persecuted by the Umayyad and 'Abbāsid caliphs, the doctrine of the Twelver Shī'ites became in the sixteenth century the official religion of Persia, where the martyrdom of Ḥusain is celebrated in most moving fashion, where the Shah rules in the name of the hidden imām, and where under the Safavids two horses were always kept ready saddled for the return of the Mahdi, or righteous king, and Jesus.

Political movements have grown out of Shī'ite principles or have adroitly made use of them. This happened especially with the Ismā'ilis. They recognize only six of the imāms and then take, as seventh, Ismā'il, although according to the Twelvers he was excluded from the succession by his father, Ja'far as-Ṣādiq, about 760. The Qarmatians rallied to the cause of the hidden imām the popular elements of Iraq and Arabia with their equalitarian tendencies, and organized a fraternity where it might be possible to discover one of the sources of freemasonry. Then the Fāṭimids, who claimed descent from Fāṭima and 'Ali, established in the tenth century in North Africa a kingdom which was transferred to Egypt. No longer is it a question of the designation of the imām by his authentic predecessor in the direct line from 'Ali; now it is rather the interior illumination of an initiate who proclaims the infusion of the divine spark in himself. The strangest of the Fāṭimid caliphs, Ḥākim, whose extravagant life has been described by Gérard de Nerval, went the full length and proclaimed himself God. As he disappeared mysteriously, his disciples founded in his name in the Hauran in Syria the closed community of the Druses, which still awaits his return. Others developed out of Ismā'ili and Fāṭimid ideas the extraordinary organization of the grand masters of Alamūt, the Old Men of the Mountain, the heads of the 'Assassins', who spread terror in Persia and Syria. For a long time it was with them that the Seljuqs, Saladin and the Crusaders had to struggle. Their representative today is well-known under the name of the Aga Khan. For his disciples in India, East Asia and Zanzibar he is the forty-eighth imām.

Ismā'ili doctrine placed a series of beings between God and man—universal reason, universal soul, first matter, space and time. Reason became incarnate in Adam, Noah, Abraham, Moses, Jesus, Muḥammad and Muḥammad ibn Ismā'il, the son of the seventh imām. Each of these seven prophets is followed by seven imāms, of whom the first is the companion of the prophet in question. 'Ali is the companion of Muḥammad, and is followed by his six successors down to Ismā'il. Ismā'il's son Muḥammad, who opens the seventh prophetic cycle, is followed by imāms who are in fact the Fāṭimids. Initiation into the doctrine takes place in seven stages, and includes a very allegorical interpretation of the Qur'ān, transmigration of souls (*tanāsukh*), and the return of the entire creation, at the end of the cycle, to universal reason.

The sect of the Anṣāris or Nuṣairis or Alaouites ('Alawis) of Asia Minor is still further removed from orthodox Islam, since its followers deify 'Ali. Externally he is 'Ali but in reality he is God eternal, from whom emanate the two other persons of the Trinity, Muḥammad and Salmān. The latter is the slightly mysterious and very intelligent Persian called Salmān who suggested to the Prophet the stratagem of digging a Ditch and was one of the first Companions to maintain the rights of 'Ali.

The sect of the opposite extreme from the Shī'ites is that of the Khārijites. As we have said, the more ardent supporters of 'Ali were shocked to see him accept an arbitration which implied doubts about his legitimate succession, since they held that 'the judgement belongs to God alone'. Their revolts were drowned in blood first by 'Ali then by the Umayyads. They succeeded in establishing in North Africa at Tahert-Tiaret, under the rule of the Rustamid imāms, a kingdom at once puritanical, democratic and theocratic, which was destroyed about 909 by the Fātimids. The survivors sought refuge in the desert, there to worship God freely according to their own ideas, having passed from the state of glory to the state of resistance and then to the state of secrecy. Today they form at Mzab a puritanical community which, since there is no longer an imām, is governed by scholars. They give themselves up to the nostalgic study of history and theology, while at the same time in the Sahara they exploit palm-groves and in the north they cultivate spices by an ingenious method. The extremist schools, the Azraqites and Sufrites, have today been replaced by the moderate 'Ibādites, not only in Algeria but also in Tripolitania, at Jerba, in Oman and at Zanzibar.

The 'Ibadite mosque at Ghardaia the Kharijite capital, in the Mzab.

Far from restricting the caliphate to the 'Alids, the Hāshimites and the Quraishites, they thought that it could pass by election to any believer of pure faith and upright character, even to a negro slave, but they held that the chief of the community ought to be deposed if he departed from the straight path. They do not believe in justification without works. They demand purity of conscience as a preliminary condition for prayer and do not admit degrees of faith; the man who commits a capital sin does not have less faith, but ceases altogether to be a believer. They accept only the literal interpretation of the uncreated Qur'ān. Their college of scholars has the dreaded right of excommunication (*tabri'ah*).

SCHOOLS, CURRENTS AND TENDENCIES

After what might be called 'the churches', it is necessary to indicate the main currents of Islamic tradition. As has been seen, *fiqh* or canonical jurisprudence occupied a place out of all proportion and ended by producing sterility, weakening the feeling for the Divine and encouraging a tendency to speculate and to make laws which presupposed an ideal state of affairs and had little bearing on reality. This has contributed to the sclerosis of society, especially when it was admitted that the gates of *ijtihād*, or the personal interpretation of the doctors, had been closed after the constitution of the four rites. The founders of these rites were considered as having the absolute power to form an opinion, their immediate successors as having no more than that of forming an opinion relatively to the consequences of the principles of a particular school (or rite), that is, within the framework of the school. As to the scholars of the following ages, they were no more than *muftis* giving *fatwas* or impersonal legal opinions.

One can well understand that this question is important when one remembers that *fiqh* is concerned with ritual and morals as well as of civil, criminal and public law, and of rules of hygiene and politeness. The *sharī'ah* or religious law forms a massive solid block, but one badly adapted to reality unless the spirit is discerned beyond the letter. Unless they decide to follow thoroughly the example of Muḥammad 'Abdu the jurists are in danger of losing themselves more and more in subtleties and arguments, while being obliged willy-nilly to accept the co-existence of local non-Muslim customs.

The relationship of the spiritual to the temporal, and man's adaptation to the modern world, are the great problems of contemporary Islam. While Turkey adopts the Swiss civil code and a laic constitution, and the Soviet republics with Muslim population suppress 'feudal survivals' such as polygamy, the Arab states of the Middle East and Pakistan seek rather for a just middle way; but radically Islamic currents are also apparent, like that of the Muslim Brotherhood, advocating complete strictness and maintaining that the revealed law is all-sufficient. The integral application of the Qur'ānic law and the refusal of all innovation (*bid'ah*), even 'praiseworthy', form the basis of the Wahhābi state of Sa'udi Arabia. These principles are today much modified by oil politics.

The need for theology, the science of the reality of God, does not seem to have made itself immediately felt, the Qur'ān and the

The qadi or judge. (*Mesopotamia*, 1230)

Sunna of the Companions being in principle all-sufficing. It was made necessary by the very development of meditation on the Qur'ānic texts, by the exigencies of the religious consciousness and of human reason, as well as by contacts with the Christian religion and Greek philosophy. This gave rise to the moderate Ash'arite school and the rationalist Mu'tazilite school. In practice, too, theology or *kalām* is always bound to *fiqh*, and also to the study of the Qur'ān or *tafsīr* and of Hadīth.

Ṣūfism represents a protest, at one and the same time against juridical formalism and against the worldliness resulting from the conquests. It gives primacy to the religion of the heart, to the love of God, and to the values of contemplation and asceticism (the cloak of wool, *ṣūf*), in contrast to the luxury of the Umayyads and the 'Abbāsids. It is not so much a school of passive ecstasy as a way of initiation to a traditional and metaphysical doctrine, and a method of spiritual realization (meditation, retreat, struggle against the self, litanies, poetry, music, dance and, in certain brotherhoods, games with sword and with fire). It is very original, despite its traditional character and despite adventitious Christian,

The great Sufi of the 8th century, Ibrahim ibn-Adham, as a hermit visited by the angels. (India, 17th century)

Neoplatonist and Hindu influences. The whole was planned to have for its point of departure meditation on certain Qur'ānic verses (which will be found further on), and presented something of an esoteric character. In this way the *ḥaqīqah* or 'spiritual reality' and *ṭarīqah* or 'way' of initiation complete the common exoteric law or *shari'ah* without contradicting it.

The great thinker, Ghazāli, who died in 1111, gave Ṣūfism its right to exist within Islam by moderating and at the same time enlivening orthodoxy, and by giving pride of place to mystic love over casuistry, while maintaining a just balance between tradition and intuition. The brotherhoods, which were founded from the twelfth century onwards and which came to have so much importance, gave sufism a social framework—not without falling a little into a routine or sometimes serving temporal interests. They embodied in different countries what one might call a third order of brothers or Ikhwān, many in number, who participated only in the more general activities and paid *ziyāras* or offerings (which were sometimes considerable), yet undeniably profited from their *barakah*, with its warm atmosphere of fervour and brotherhood. Popular devotion has also found great satisfaction in the cult of the saints (*awliyā'*, plural of *wali*, friends of God), which, without seceding from Islam, made it approach more nearly the infrastructures of universal religion.

On the margin of these religious currents there grew up schools of science and philosophy, which preserved, developed and transmitted the principal elements of Greek civilization (with the exception of literature in the narrow sense, poetry and drama), as well as Indian elements like the system of numbers. Corresponding to the Arabic translations from Baghdad in the eighth and ninth centuries are the translations from Arabic into Latin at Toledo in the twelfth century.

Although appearing to oppose each other philosophy and sufism were the two great poles of Islamic culture, at times warring externally with each other but at bottom complementing and mutually enriching one another and enriching the intellectual and social life. The great Almohad sovereigns, who admitted the allegorical interpretation of the Qur'ān as well as the rationalism of the philosophers, at first favoured both of them. In course of time, however, the equilibrium was upset, for Ya'qūb al-Manṣūr, going to war and needing scholars, kept aloof from both the mystics and Ibn Rushd (Averroes), to the profit of the doctors of the law. Sūfism took the form of brotherhoods and maraboutism, and philosophy emigrated to Europe. The glorious names of al-Rāzi (Rhazes), al-Kindi, al-Fārābi, al-Bīrūni, Ibn Sīnā (Avicenna), Ibn Zuhr, Ibn Rushd and Ibn Tufail mark out this great period of Arab science, which rendered so many services to civilization. The culminating point was the great commentary on Aristotle undertaken by Ibn Rushd at the request of the Almohad caliph, and its influence can be seen in the scholastics and Saint Thomas Aquinas. By his theory of the three degrees of intellect, which recalls in its own way the esotericism of the sufis, Ibn Rushd had confirmed the supreme agreement between high Reason and the dogmas of a religion which was revealed but was without 'mysteries' properly speaking. Ghazāli was opposed to Avicenna and philosophers like Pascal and Descartes, but this opposition was perhaps superficial rather than profound. The general eclipse of both mystics and philosophers, which limited all spiritual and intellectual activity to formal juridical speculation, marked the beginning of the decadence—which Ibn Khaldūn in the fourteenth century was to analyse in a general way with the clinical lucidity of a Montaigne or a Montesquieu. The decadence even showed itself in literature, which had been so rich from the seventh to the thirteenth centuries, but which from that time until the renaissance at the end of the nineteenth century only contains a small number of great names.

Bronze lion.
(Spain, 11th century)

THE RENAISSANCE

The renaissance or *nahḍah*, stimulated by European influences, can be seen in literature and religion. The great problem, and the most agonizing one at times in actual experience, is to reconcile tradition and the modern way of life. Writers must aim at a style adapted to new needs, at infusing fresh life into traditional genres and at creating something new in the realm of the novel and the theatre. Arab culture must be reintegrated into world culture. There must, moreover, be a return in one sense to the authentic sources of the great classical period of the ninth to twelfth centuries.

Would we be digressing too much from our subject if we were to say a word about the special difficulties confronting contemporary Arab writers? They were described some years ago by Bishr Farès,* and are not the least of the problems which present-day Muslims have to solve. Some of their aspects are sufficiently important for us to pause a moment before proceeding to the other main problems, including those which concern the family and the general religious attitude towards tradition.

Let us take first the difficulties of language and style. As we know, the spoken language is different from the written language. Until recent times, apart from popular or semi-popular poems which were generally sung, the idea never occurred of writing anything at all except in the manner of classical Arabic; and the tendency to write in dialect, except for theatre and radio, or only for certain parts of the dialogue, had scarcely come into being. The written language, incomparably richer and more expressive, also gained some of its prestige from the fact that it is the language of the Qur'ān. It is the liturgical language, not only of the Muslims, but also of the Christians (mass may be said in Arabic but not in French or English!). At the moment the process of evolution is not developing as in Europe in the fifteenth and sixteenth centuries.

* *Des difficultés d'ordre linguistique, culturel et social que rencontre un écrivain arabe moderne:* Revue des Études Islamiques, 1936, iii, 221–246.

Then, literary vernaculars like English grew up alongside of Latin, which had previously been the only language of the scholars. In Arabic there would rather appear to be a certain fusion between the literary and the spoken language, each one necessarily enriching the other, since the latter is little more than a syntactical simplification of the former.

It is invariably true that vocabulary is badly suited to modern times; sometimes it is too rich, sometimes too poor. Controversialists who were neither very observant nor very well informed have put forward the theory that the conception of love is unknown to the Arab. But the lexicographers can produce an enormous number of synonyms and of words expressing different shades of meaning and different degrees of feeling. For example: *ḥubb*, love; *maḥabbah*, reciprocal love, divine love; *'ishq*, desire; *shawq*, ardent desire; *hawā*, lively inclination; *kalaf*, amorous ardour; *gharām*, passion; *sha'af*, burning of the heart; *law'ah* and *lā'ij*, devouring love; *tabl*, when the lover becomes ill with love; *tā'im*, when the lover is enslaved by love; *tadlīh*, when the lover loses his reason; *huyūm*, when the lover is distraught and wandering. It requires considerable skill if a writer is to handle such a vocabulary without becoming too wordy, vague and unaesthetic. On the one hand, a profuse vocabulary is given over to obsolete types of life, to the desert of the ancient Arabs. On the other hand, the language lacks terms for the life of the present day, and will have to transpose or transcribe from foreign non-semitic languages. This cannot be brought about without considerable artificiality and clumsiness.

As for the style, it must break away from the early archaic models, like models turgid with the classicism of a decadent era, in order to find a direct and living style in the tradition of a Jāḥiz, a Ma'arri and an Ibn ar-Rūmi. It is not without difficulty that one tries to subordinate form to matter. As for the matter, the thought is far from being perfectly simple. Tolerance is ample enough; there is no inquisition nor Holy Office. Social pressure is not increased, as in certain societies, by a press with stentorian voice or a one-way public opinion. None the less the social pressure is evident. The writings of Ṭaha Ḥusain provoked ministerial crises before their author ever became minister; and the fundamental book of shaykh 'Ali 'Abd ar-Rāziq on public law, opening the way for a separation of the spiritual and the temporal, began by being condemned by the ulemas. Also frowned on were the writings of Qāsim Amin in Egypt and of Ṭāhir al-Ḥaddād in

Tunisia on the emancipation of women. Anything which touches on the origins of Islam, or which concerns the Prophet and the Qur'ān, is dangerous ground. Perhaps there is even some satisfaction to be gained from relying on non-Muslim authors to look after historical criticism when they do so with sufficient objectivity and sympathy.

When Bishr Farès wrote his famous article he also emphasized the gap between authors and their public, the social and material difficulties, and the difficulty that poets and prose writers have in detaching themselves from romanticism and from an excited admiration for 'Paul et Virginie', Lamartine and 'Sous les Tilleuls'. Things have changed a lot in the last twenty years. Novelists and poets evolve easily through all shades of realism and surrealism. Only the public now remains fixed, and does not provide a very vast field nor a very substantial platform. It is even rather moving.

Moving, too, and often tragic is the effort to adapt the moral, social and religious ways of life. We have said that canon law is stifling where the intellectual effort is given up which draws the consequences from the principles, which permits adaptability and prevents the sacrifice of the spirit to the letter, the sacrifice of life to the shell produced by a school at a certain period and claimed to be definitive.

This is a burning matter, and a particularly acute one where woman and the family are concerned. Like most Semitic societies the Muslims have a patriarchal constitution, and have not yet found the point of equilibrium. The situation with regard to woman and the family has created for Muslim society a serious handicap, of which it is more or less aware, which it sometimes tries to deny, and from which it sometimes tries to free itself.

For thousands of years humanity has tried numerous ways of resolving sexual and family problems. Ethnography and sociology have taught us to regard them with a certain relativity, and it is always necessary to keep in mind the differences between theory and practice, between the ideal and reality. In this respect the question of adaptation is always unavoidable. What is good and possible in one age and under certain conditions may be no longer so in another period. Life does not tolerate laziness or permit standing still; just as fortunes which do not increase grow less, so sclerosis has to be dearly paid for. The three main points are polygamy, the right of *jabr* and unilateral divorce. Contrary to popular belief the first is by no means the most important. Even

Ibn-Sa'ud

more than polygamy, which is becoming less and less common (except among the black sultans of the Sudan and reactionary types like Ibn Sa'ūd), automatic and arbitrary divorce by a single word from the husband is the great scourge of Muslim family life, 'an intolerable scandal' as Professor Bousquet puts it.* It ruins the stability of the family, and has disastrous results both for the psychology of the parents and the education of the children.

As for the right of *jabr*, which permits giving minors in marriage without consulting them, it runs contrary to the idea of a union by free consent. It favours unions at too early an age to be good physiologically or morally; but it should be possible to remedy this easily enough. It is primarily a question of custom.

The father of feminism in the Orient was Qāsim Amīn, who died in 1908, a follower, like Muḥammad 'Abduh, of the ardent reformer Al-Afghāni. His 'New Woman' in 1901 opened the controversy, and his posthumous book, *Kalimāt*, bears witness to the same preoccupations. During this time Madame Sha'rāwi founded the Women's Union and edited the review *L'Egyptienne* in Arabic and French. In Tunisia a leader of the first Destour, Ṭāhir al-Ḥaddād, who worked for a modernistic, anti-Wahhābite outlook and who died in 1934, published in 1930 *Our Women in Law and in Society*† to point out the need for basic reforms and their accord with Islam properly understood. The lawyers, he maintained, had been responsible for aggravating matters instead of easing them. It was not Islam that was responsible but the

*G. H. Bousquet, *Du droit musulman et de son application effective dans le monde*, Algiers, 1949.

†There is a very detailed analysis in *Revue des Études Islamiques*, 1935, third part, pp. 201–230.

Muslims and the doctors, who were fiercely intent on aiding the letter and killing the spirit. Entrenched behind the alleged prohibition of *ijtihād* the literalists, he maintains, have degraded Muslim society. They have facilitated divorce at a time when the church frowns at it; they have encouraged polygamy while the Qur'ān, though tolerating it, disapproves of it and upholds inseparable conjugal affection; they only prescribe the indemnity for legal retirement, and pass over in silence the indemnity for divorce.

His merciless sociological and psychological analyses showed the disastrous effects of child marriage, of the right of *jabr*, of close confinement and of the veil (in the broad sense; we are not thinking of the article of dress). But people prefer to be flattered, and Ṭāhir al-Haddād had little success. The seed, however, had been sown.

A glance at the state of the law in this respect in different countries allows us to pinpoint the results of these efforts, and will show us very varied situations. In Sa'udi Arabia they have tried to put the clock back, enforcing in all its strictness the Ḥanbalite code as further exaggerated by the Wahhābite sect. They cut off a thief's hand. They forbid alcohol, tobacco and the cult of saints. The king has given a lead with his large harem. Certain measures, however, have been taken against slavery.

At the other extreme many states have secularized the law of personal status. Turkey has adopted almost in its entirety the Swiss Civil Code. The Muslims of the U.S.S.R. and of Albania are under the ordinary law, and the Soviet regime combats all 'feudal survivals'.

The haik and the ajar of Algiers allow only the eyes and the forehead to be seen.

In Syria and the Lebanon Muslims are under the Ḥanafite code modified by various Turkish laws, which are opposed to marriage before puberty and to the right of *jabr*, which go so far as to demand, since 1917, a medical certificate before marriage, which have recourse to the Ḥanbalite and Mālikite rites to enable the woman to institute a suit for divorce, and which require formal divorce procedure.

In Egypt, too, there has been recourse to the choice between rites and likewise to the limitation of the competence of the judge by that of the sovereign. The age of marriage has been fixed at eighteen for males and sixteen for females, thus automatically abolishing the right of *jabr* which in the Ḥanafite rite is not recognized after puberty. The law provides for obligatory registration, for divorce at the instance of the woman, and for guarantees against arbitrary divorce. The year 1956 was to have seen the suppression or control of religious courts, which to begin with would have led to a secularization of status for Christians, Muslims and Jews. But the matter is not yet settled.

Persian law fixes the ages at eighteen and fifteen, and requires consent. Our knowledge of the recent changes in Yugoslavia, Indonesia and Pakistan is scanty.

In North Africa the situation until now has been stationary. In Morocco strict Mālikite law regulated that part of the country not under customary law (the mountainous and Berber part). But the Sultan has shown himself favourable to the emancipation of women and this has been one of the points in the programme of the Istiqlāl since their recent congress. In Algeria the qādi has been told not to deal with the contract for the marriage of a girl of less than fifteen, this age being regarded as making it quite certain puberty has occurred. But the document of the qādi is not always in practice an indispensable condition, and one still hears of girls of thirteen and fourteen being married, though it is true that this is becoming more and more rare. Family allowances will have the certain result of promoting registration at mahkamas and town-halls. In Kabylia, where customary personal status is in force, which differs from Muslim status and is very unfavourable to the woman (especially when it is alleged to be applicable even outside the normal social setting), the law of 2 May 1930 fixes the age of marriage for a girl at fifteen.

Arbitrary divorce acts cruelly, and, except among the middle-class bourgeoisie, stable households are the exception rather than the rule. Divorce is, in effect, much more convenient and much less costly than polygamy. In Algeria it has fallen to 3 per cent for the whole country, to 1 per cent for the large towns, and the rate is steadily becoming lower.

A remarkable effort was made by the Commission of Codification on the initiative of Dean Morand.* Skilfully making use of the appeal to various rites, of the principle of public welfare, of the most solid Islamic authorities, and of the Qur'ān and the Ḥadīth in their spirit and in their letter, the draft of the code made the following notable declaration: 'Article 2. The validity of marriage presupposes the fulfilment of the following conditions: (1) both parties must have reached the age of puberty; (2) there must be proof of consent; (3) no hindrance must be present; (4) a dowry must be fixed; (5) the prescribed formalities must be observed.'

Morand's code did not come into force. The initiative shown by him was not followed; and besides this, neither the Muslims nor the French seemed to think much of it. It is a sad paradox to see three 'French departments' less advanced in this respect than Syria and Egypt.

We have delayed somewhat over this crucial question. It is the chief social aspect of the general intellectual and religious attitude in face of the principles of the Islamic tradition. The great reformer Muḥammad 'Abduh, breaking with the principle of *taqlīd* or argument from authority (or servile imitation), resolutely re-opened the gates of *ijtihād* at the beginning of the century, as we have said. His admirable *Risālat at-Tawḥīd* truly brought about a revival of theology, just as the writings of al-Ghazāli had done eight centuries earlier. The possibility became apparent of a humanistic evolution, loosening the bonds of the spiritual and the temporal, and launching itself resolutely along the path of progress. Despite the courage of certain intellectual heirs of the master, these possibilities have not yet been fully exploited, though they would lead to a religious and social renaissance in the face of a sclerosis which is in fact more of an enemy to authentic and living tradition than the excesses of modernism themselves. The reform movement, liberal at first, tends above all to adopt an attitude of purist return to theoretical sources, and this produces afresh a predominance of formalism over the mystical currents, and a

***Avant-projet de Code présenté à la commission de codification du droit musulman algérien* by Marcel Morand. Algiers, 1916 (543 pages).

stiffening of dogmatic and juridical positions at the expense of the forces of evolution. As to the movement of the Muslim Brotherhood, after spreading abroad the burning words of its founder, it seems to be sliding, in accordance with the acute analysis of Péguy, from mysticism towards politics.

Islam, now (in 1958) in the year 1377 of its era, would, in a word, have to achieve the same intellectual and social effort as has been made in Europe since the sixteenth century, but without falling into the same errors. For what happened in Europe the Christian churches, despite certain immediate appearances to the contrary, are ultimately better off; they have greater freedom over against kings, states, and classes; theology has advanced when it has avoided rigidity on certain points; the masses have been recovered after out-of-date ties have been broken. For Islam this would be a new 'revival of the religious sciences'; but, as François Bonjean suggested, it is necessary for it to choose and discriminate between living tradition and rotten tradition.

This is how the problem presents itself. The decadence of Muslim religious thought, practically limited to *fiqh*, is only equalled by the devout fervour and the amazing sureness of faith. Intellectual activity is almost entirely concerned with problems of jurisprudence and casuistry; ignorance of philosophy and of classical and modern literature is nearly complete. It is not surprising that this lack of culture is reflected in religion, depriving it of the best of its forces. The great rites remain intact, strictly fixed for ever—the rites of prayer, the witness to the Unity of God, fasting—but these rites, caught up in their formalism, have come to be part of a static religion. Superstition, the fruit of ignorance, was rife; often very paralysing, it is nevertheless sometimes perhaps less arid than the arguments of the lawyers, for they were often only the popular spontaneous expression of spiritual realities.

While attacking the fundamental *taqlīd* at the root of the evil, the first reformers made a vigorous drive to combat superstition. This, therefore, took first place, for it is easier to criticize in a negative fashion what deserves criticism, than to exercise creative thought freely. In an attempt to get back to the sources—which is the myth, the source of action of many of the reformers—they opposed *bida'āt* or innovations. Some reformers ended up by allowing themselves to be too strongly hypnotized by these *bida'āt*, so much so, that in trying to hunt for innovations, they became involved in the condemnation of all evolution, and returned to a purely conservative attitude. Instead of remaining a source of progress, this body of reform—even in the most moderate trends, those which adopted the titles of *salafi* or follower of the 'fathers' and *iṣlāḥi* or purist—was itself in danger of becoming rigid. During this period the Wahhābite puritanism showed a complete reaction on the spiritual plane, and a very material, political and economic adaptation on the temporal plane. In Turkey, on the other hand, Kemalist secularism broke with traditional Islam and resorted to surgery rather than to

Mustafa Kemal.

medicine—one way of resolving a problem is to suppress the elements of it.

Today two tendencies face each other, generally speaking; both of them could become forces of progress and of spiritual life, but in fact each tends in its own way to be retrograde; a new synthesis is still to be found. What are generally termed the '*ulamā*, especially in Algeria, the followers of the zealous and noble Ben Badis, are fighting against superstition and illiteracy; they found schools, try to develop an Arab and Qur'ānic culture, and give themselves up to spreading instruction. But they tend to believe that traditional Islam, after a slight attempt to tidy it up, is self-sufficient. They look down on secular civilization, they account perfect the

Tombs of saints in the Mzab (Melika)

City tombs (Sidi ʻAbd ar-Rahman, Algiers).

law of personal status, they are not interested in the emancipation of women, and they combine all their efforts in a struggle against their enemies the marabouts and the brotherhoods, whom they consider to be the agents of obscurantism and even colonialism. Some of their criticism is justified; but it may well be that the worthy 'marabouts', so much decried, yet more pliant and more moderate, are more open to progress, just as in the past they were often the champions of toleration. They still do a great deal for the poor, though at times they also hold them to ransom a little; in the case of those who are honest, however, this is in compensation for material aid to the poorest and for moral aid to many. 'Here you feel you are no longer forgotten,' I was told by a workman from a suburb of Algiers whom I met at the annual reunion of a brotherhood in the province of Oran.

If we try to see at a turning point in history how decadence has operated, it will help us to see how to correct it. In 1169 the Almohad caliph Abu Ya'qūb Yusūf summoned Averroes to Marrakesh. Rather disturbed at first, the latter at last understood that the caliph was about to adopt the bold ideas of the philosophers. It was at the ruler's own wish that he undertook his great commentary on Aristotle. Besides, the Almohad dynasty had founded itself on a doctrine, that of Ibn Tumart, which allowed an allegorical interpretation of the Qur'ān—this opened many windows—and reacted against the formalism of the fuqahā', which alone the preceding Almoravid dynasty had protected. Unfortunately the third Almohad, Abu Yūsuf Ya'qūb, for whom the battle of Alcaros (1196) was to gain the title of al-Mansūr (the

Procession to a sacred waterfall, in the Atlas.
In the background, the white dome of a marabout.

Victorious), needed for this campaign what might be called spiritual forces, and called upon the fuqahā'. He sent Averroes into temporary exile and had his books burnt, just as the Almoravids had burnt those of al-Ghazāli. The liberal free-thinking philosophers and the Ṣūfis or mystics were likewise condemned. Now these two schools were the living forces in the Muslim civilization of the time. They balanced one another and made progress possible. Their elimination or their eclipse brought about that of authentic living culture. Philosophy emigrated to Europe, and it was Saint Thomas Aquinas who profited from Averroes' commentary on Aristotle. Ṣūfism took refuge in the brotherhoods, and sank into maraboutism in the narrow sense.

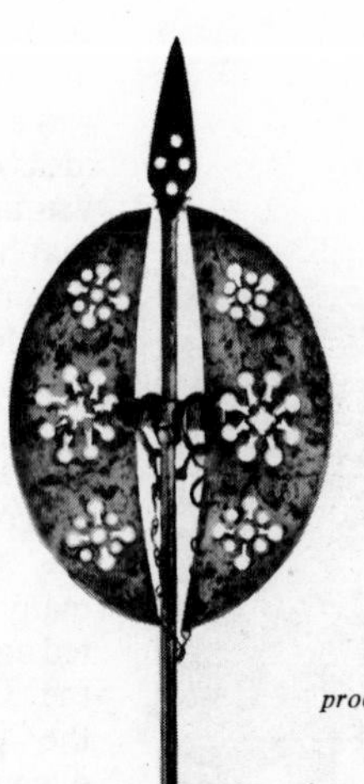

Double axe used in the processions of the Hamadcha. (Moulay-Idriss, Morocco)

HUMANISM AND 'OPEN' RELIGION

Today modern European thought plays in the *nahḍah* (renaissance) the role played by the *falsafa* (philosophy, especially that of the Arabic Neoplatonists) in the twelfth century; and it is up to the living forces of religious thought to provide an 'open' and dynamic mystique. The bases for it exist. Islam, which has contributed to the spiritual life of humanity and has enriched its culture, offers permanent values from which all have profited. 'Intermediate nation' as the Qur'ān says, it has its role to play between east and west. If it has, like all religions and moral codes, its 'closed' and 'static' aspects in the Bergsonian sense, it also has what is needed for an 'open' religion.

Tradition relates that the Prophet said: 'Work for this world as if you were always to live in it, and for the next world as if you were to die tomorrow.'

The first ḥadīth in Bukhārī's collection is the affirmation of this 'open' and anti-formalist aspect: 'Acts are judged by the intention.' If a man does not give up lying and evil-doing God has no need of his fast, it is also said. 'The best is he who is first reconciled. A man is a true Muslim when no other Muslim has anything to fear from either his tongue or his hand. A man is a true Emigrant when he flees from what God has forbidden to him.'

The Prophet having said one day: 'Help your Muslim brother, whether he is oppressor or oppressed,' some one in astonishment said: 'I am ready to help my oppressed brother; but how am I to help the oppressor?' 'By hindering him doing wrong' was the answer.

As for the Qur'ān, it declares that to kill a man is the same as killing all men, and to save a single man is the same as saving the whole human race (v, 35); that piety does not consist merely in turning towards the east or the west, but in having faith, in giving to the poor for the love of God, in praying, in ransoming prisoners, in keeping promises and in patiently bearing one's trials (ii, 172).

It asserts that 'the flesh and blood of sacrifices do not reach to God, but your piety reaches Him' (xxii, 38); and that there is 'no constraint in religion' (ii, 257). It counsels: 'Render good for evil, and you shall see your adversary change into a protector and a friend (xli, 34). It stigmatizes pride, and affirms the unity and solidarity of the human race, the rights of conscience and the worth of the individual. The impassioned affirmation of divine omnipotence frees man from man, guaranteeing the dignity of the individual, since he cannot feel himself to be the slave of any other slave of this awful, ever-present God. (*'Abd* signifies servant, slave, worshipper.) The intense consciousness of the Absolute puts all that is relative in its proper perspective.

'God does not love the oppressors' (xlii, 38). 'Justice is next to piety' (v, 11). 'Do not walk proudly on the earth' (xvii, 39). Mankind, divided into tribes and families, has been 'created from a single individual,' and 'the worthiest is he who fears God most' (vi, 98; vii, 189; xlix, 13). The differences of race are only a 'lesson for the worlds' (xxx, 21). And the ḥadīth proclaim that 'an Arab is not superior to a foreigner, nor a white man to a black man, except by reason of his piety', since God has sent His raḥmah, His mercy and goodness, to all races, 'to the red and to the black'.

ÉMILE DERMENGHEM

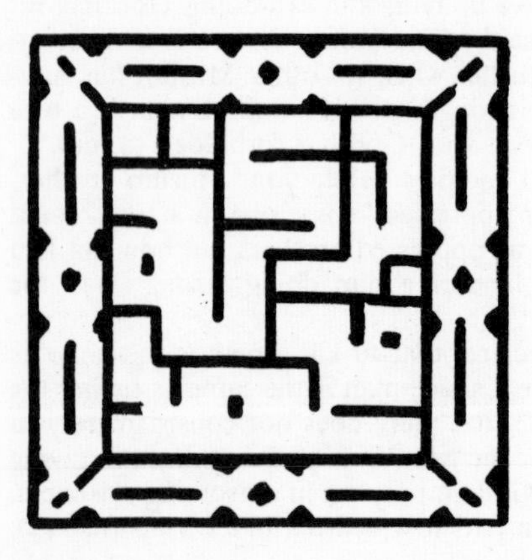

Kufic rectangle, reading Barakat Muhammad, 'The benediction of Muhammad!'

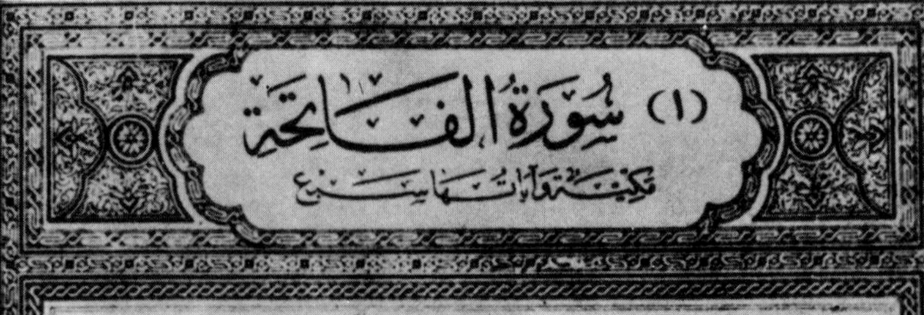

بِسْمِ ٱللَّهِ ٱلرَّحْمَٰنِ ٱلرَّحِيمِ ﴿١﴾

ٱلْحَمْدُ لِلَّهِ رَبِّ ٱلْعَٰلَمِينَ ﴿٢﴾ ٱلرَّحْمَٰنِ ٱلرَّحِيمِ ﴿٣﴾

مَٰلِكِ يَوْمِ ٱلدِّينِ ﴿٤﴾ إِيَّاكَ نَعْبُدُ وَإِيَّاكَ

نَسْتَعِينُ ﴿٥﴾ ٱهْدِنَا ٱلصِّرَٰطَ ٱلْمُسْتَقِيمَ ﴿٦﴾

صِرَٰطَ ٱلَّذِينَ أَنْعَمْتَ عَلَيْهِمْ غَيْرِ ٱلْمَغْضُوبِ

عَلَيْهِمْ وَلَا ٱلضَّآلِّينَ ﴿٧﴾

In the name of God, the merciful and compassionate, Praise be to God, the Lord of the worlds, the merciful, the compassionate, the king of the day of judgement. Thee do we worship, and of thee do we beg assistance. Direct us in the right way, in the way of those to whom thou hast been gracious; not of those against whom thou art incensed, nor of those who go astray.
The Fatihah (first sura of the Qur'an)

TEXTS*

THE QUR'ĀN

As we have seen, the Qur'ān cannot be considered as a literary production of which Muḥammad is the author. Its value and its very beauty raise it in a fashion above literature, both because of its origin and because of the character attributed to it. The full effect of a work of art and of this one in particular is the result of a contact and a collaboration between the thought out of which it issues and the thought which receives it. The Qur'ān is an 'inspired' book. It is at least so because it is not the mere fruit of the conscious discursive thought of Muḥammad or because his consciousness was in a peculiar state of which there were various degrees, but which was always distinguishable from the normal state, and which was then linked to his deep sub-conscious. In some cases it was no doubt personal, but at the same time (one may believe) immersed in a reality which transcended the phenomenal world.

On the other hand, the Qur'ān is considered as the uncreated word of God, and because of this is recited during the formal prayers so as to enable the worshippers through this spoken word to enter into communion with the eternal Word, and this prevents us from treating it as if it were a poem. Like all sacred books, even when they deal with historical facts, with law, or with trivial questions of the day, it is necessary to apply to it rules of interpretation. In this way there will be several different meanings for a given verse, and one at least will always be 'true'.

NOTE BY THE TRANSLATOR

* The texts have been translated from the French and not from the originals. The Qur'ān, however, has been given in the translation of George Sale, but this has often been modified to bring it more into harmony with the French version.

The recitation of the Qur'ān has not only a liturgical and sacramental value but also a mystical one. It sets before each soul eternal realities of which the soul already has potentially a 'memory' (in a platonic sense). The word dhikr *repeated several times in the Qur'ān means at the same time recitation, thought and memory.*

The Qur'ān has no chronological order, it is expansive, it bursts out according to circumstances, it often repeats itself, sometimes contradicts itself (thus leading to the curious theory that some verses have been abrogated by others), and yet despite it all it is dynamic. We give here some verses which are significant from the point of view of theology, ethics and eschatology, then the stories of Abraham, Moses, Jesus and Mary which are the framework of the 'religion of the prophets', and finally some verses of a mythical and mystical turn which have been a foundation for the spiritual flights of the Ṣūfis, and have often been quoted and expounded by them.

ٱللَّهُ لَآ إِلَـٰهَ إِلَّا هُوَ ٱلْحَىُّ ٱلْقَيُّومُ

لَا تَأْخُذُهُۥ سِنَةٌ وَلَا نَوْمٌ لَّهُۥ مَا فِى ٱلسَّمَـٰوَٰتِ وَمَا فِى ٱلْأَرْضِ

مَن ذَا ٱلَّذِى يَشْفَعُ عِندَهُۥٓ إِلَّا بِإِذْنِهِۦ يَعْلَمُ مَا بَيْنَ أَيْدِيهِمْ

وَمَا خَلْفَهُمْ وَلَا يُحِيطُونَ بِشَىْءٍ مِّنْ عِلْمِهِۦٓ إِلَّا بِمَا شَآءَ

وَسِعَ كُرْسِيُّهُ ٱلسَّمَـٰوَٰتِ وَٱلْأَرْضَ وَلَا يَـُٔودُهُۥ حِفْظُهُمَا

وَهُوَ ٱلْعَلِىُّ ٱلْعَظِيمُ

The verse of the throne. (*K.* 2, 256)
The translation is given opposite at the beginning of the Sura of the Cow

Sura of the Cow*

God! there is no God but he; the living, the self-subsisting: neither slumber nor sleep seizeth him; to him belongeth whatsoever is in heaven, and on earth. Who is he that can intercede with him, but through his good pleasure? He knoweth that which is past, and that which is to come unto them, and they shall not comprehend anything of his knowledge, but so far as he pleaseth. His throne is extended over heaven and earth, and the preservation of both is no burden unto him. He is the high, the mighty. (ii, 256)

It is not righteousness that ye turn your faces in prayer towards the east and the west, but righteousness is of him who believeth in God and the last day, and the angels, and the scriptures, and the prophets; who giveth money for God's sake unto his kindred, and unto orphans, and the needy, and the stranger, and those who ask, and for redemption of captives; who is constant at prayer, and giveth alms; and of those who perform their covenant, when they have covenanted, and who behave themselves patiently in adversity, and hardships, and in time of violence: these are they who are true, and these are they who fear God. (ii, 172)

The present life was ordained for those who believe not, and they laugh the faithful to scorn; but they who fear God shall be above them, on the day of the resurrection: for God is bountiful unto whom he pleaseth without measure. Mankind was of one faith, and God sent prophets bearing good tidings, and denouncing threats, and sent down with them the scripture in truth, that it might judge between men of that concerning which they disagreed; and none disagreed concerning it, except those to whom the same scriptures were delivered, after the declarations of God's will had come unto them, out of envy among themselves. And God directed those who believed, to that truth concerning which they disagreed, by his will: for God directeth whom he pleaseth unto the right way. Did ye think ye should enter paradise, when as yet no such thing had happened unto you, as hath happened unto those who have been before you? They suffered calamity and tribulation, and were afflicted; so that the apostle, and they who believeth with him, said, When will the help of God come? Is not the help of God nigh? (ii, 208–210)

---

*The name of this sura comes from verses 63ff. which speak of the sacrifice of a cow by Moses on the occasion of a murder.

Sura of the Pilgrimage*

It is God who has caused you to live and will cause you to die and then will bring you to life again. In truth man is ungrateful. (xxii, 65)

Sura of the Spider†

Say, Go through the earth, and see how he originally produceth creatures: afterwards will God reproduce another production; for God is almighty. (xxix, 19)

Sura of the Kneelers‡

Say, God giveth you life; and afterwards causeth you to die: hereafter will he assemble you together on the day of resurrection: there is no doubt thereof; but the greater part of men do not understand. (xlv, 25)

Sura of Noah§

God hath also produced and caused you to spring forth from the earth: hereafter he will cause you to return into the same; and he will again take you thence. (lxxi, 16–17)

Sura of Consultation||

Whatever things are given you, they are the provision of this present life: but the reward which is with God is better and more durable, for those who believe and put their trust in their Lord;

---

*The name of this sura comes from certain verses dealing with the pilgrimage.

†The name of this sura comes from verse 40, 'Those who take patrons apart from God resemble the spider which makes itself a house. It is the most fragile of houses.'

‡The name of this sura comes from verse 27, 'Thou shalt see all the people kneeling.'

§This sura recounts the story of Noah.

||This sura advises consultation about important matters (verse 36).

and who avoid heinous and filthy crimes, and when they are angry, forgive; and who hearken unto their Lord, and are constant at prayer, and whose affairs are directed by consultation among themselves, and who give alms out of what we have bestowed on them; and who, when an injury is done them, avenge themselves (and the retaliation of evil ought to be an evil proportionate thereto): but he who forgiveth, and is reconciled unto his enemy, shall receive his reward from God; for he loveth not the unjust doers. And whoso shall avenge himself, after he hath been injured; as to these, it is not lawful to punish them for it: but it is only lawful to punish those who wrong men, and act insolently in the earth, against justice; these shall suffer a grievous punishment. And whoso beareth injuries patiently, and forgiveth; verily this is a necessary work. (xlii, 34–41)

Sura of the Evident Sign*

They who believe and do good works, these are the best of creatures: their reward with their Lord shall be gardens of perpetual abode, through which rivers flow; they shall remain therein for ever. God will be well pleased in them; and they shall be well pleased in him. This is prepared for him who shall fear his Lord. (xcviii, 6–8)

Sura of the Separated†

He who doth right, doth it to the advantage of his own soul; and he who doth evil, doth it against the same: for thy Lord is not unjust towards his servants. (xli, 46)

Good and evil shall not be held equal. Turn away evil with that which is better; and behold, the man between whom and thyself there was enmity shall become, as it were, thy protector and friend. (xli, 34)

---

*The name is derived from verse 1, 'The Evident Sign is the Qur'ān recited by the Prophet.'

†The name is derived from verse 2, 'it is a Book whose verses are clearly separated.'

Sura of the Cave*

Wealth and children are the ornament of this present life; but good works, which are permanent, are better in the sight of thy Lord, with respect to the reward, and better with respect to hope. (xviii, 44)

Sura of the Table†

He who slayeth a soul, which hath not slain a soul, or committed wickedness in the earth, shall be as if he had slain all mankind: but he who saveth a soul alive, shall be as if he had saved the lives of all mankind. (v, 35)

Sura of the Cow

Remember me, and I will remember you, and give thanks unto me, and be not unbelievers. O true believers, beg assistance with patience and prayer, for God is with the patient. And say not of those who are slain in fight for the religion of God, that they are dead; yea, they are living: but ye do not understand. We will surely prove you by afflicting you in some measure with fear, and hunger, and decrease of wealth, and loss of lives, and scarcity of fruits: but bear good tidings unto the patient, who, when a misfortune befalleth them, say, We are God's, and unto him shall we surely return. Upon them shall be blessings from their Lord and mercy, and they are the rightly directed. (ii, 147–152)

---

*The name is derived from the well-known legend of the Seven Sleepers recounted in verses 8–25.

†The name comes from verses 112ff., describing the miraculous food given by Jesus to his disciples (Eucharist?).

Sura of the Folding Up*

When the sun shall be folded up;
When the stars shall fall;
When the mountains shall be made to pass away;
When the camels ten months gone with young shall be neglected;
When the wild beasts shall be gathered together;
When the seas shall boil;
When the souls shall be joined again to their bodies:
When the girl who hath been buried alive shall be asked
For what crime she was put to death;
When the books shall be laid open;
When the heaven shall be removed;
When hell shall burn fiercely;
When paradise shall be brought near;
Every soul shall know what it hath wrought. (lxxxi, 1–14)

*So called from the first verse.

Hell. Muhammad in the foreground, while red demons transfix men with lances. (Book of the Assumption, Turkish ms., B.N.)

Sura of the Earthquake

When the earth shall be shaken by an earthquake,
And the earth shall cast forth her burdens;
And a man shall say, What aileth her?
On that day the earth shall declare her tidings,
For that day thy Lord will inspire her.
On that day men shall go forward in distinct classes, that they may behold their works.
And whoever shall have wrought good of the weight of an ant, shall behold the same.
And whosoever shall have wrought evil of the weight of an ant, shall behold the same. (xcix)

The archangel Israfil and the trumpet of the Last Judgement. Iran, about 1400)

Paradise.
Muhammad, guided by the angel Gabriel, sees the houris of the Garden.
(*Turkish ms., B.N.*)

Sura of the Inevitable Event*

Reposing on couches adorned with gold and precious stones, sitting opposite to one another thereon. Youths which shall continue in their bloom for ever, shall go round about to attend them, with goblets, and beakers, and a cup of flowing wine: their heads shall not ache by drinking the same, neither shall their reason be disturbed: and with fruits of the sorts which they shall choose, and the flesh of birds of the kind which they shall desire. And there shall accompany them fair damsels having large black eyes; resembling pearls hidden in their shells: as a reward for that which they shall have wrought. They shall not hear therein any vain discourse, or any charge of sin; but only the salutation, Peace! Peace! (lvi, 15–25)

*This eschatological sura is one of the oldest, and portrays the Last Judgement as the inevitable event.

Abraham. (Modern popular picture, Algiers)

ABRAHAM

Sura of the Cattle*

It is he who hath created the heavens and the earth in truth; and whenever he saith unto a thing, Be, it is. His word is the truth; and his will be the kingdom on the day whereon the trumpet shall be sounded: he knoweth whatever is secret, and whatever is public; he is the wise, the knowing. Call to mind when Abraham said unto his father, Azar, Dost thou take images for gods? Verily I perceive that thou and thy people are in a manifest error. And thus did did we show unto Abraham the kingdom of heaven and earth, that he might become one of those who firmly believe. And when the night overshadowed him, he saw a star, and he said, This is my Lord; but when it set, he said, I like not gods which set. And

*So called from verses 137ff. which describe Arab superstitions about animals.

when he saw the moon rising, he said, This is my Lord; but when he saw it set, he said, Verily if my Lord direct me not, I shall become one of the people who go astray. And when he saw the sun rising, he said, This is my Lord, this is the greatest; but when it set, he said, O my people, verily I am clear of that which ye associate with God: I direct my face unto him who hath created the heavens and the earth; I am orthodox, and am not one of the idolaters. And his people disputed with him: and he said, Will ye dispute with me concerning God? Since he hath now directed me, and I fear not that which ye associate with him, unless that my Lord willeth a thing; for my Lord comprehendeth all things by his knowledge: will ye not therefore consider? And how should I fear that which ye associate with God, since ye fear not to have associated with God that concerning which he hath sent down unto you no authority? which therefore of the two parties is the more safe, if ye understand aright? They who believe, and clothe not their faith with injustice, they shall enjoy security, and they are rightly directed. And this is our argument wherewith we furnished Abraham that he might make use of it against his people: we exalt unto degrees of wisdom and knowledge whom we please; for thy Lord is wise and knowing. (vi, 72–83)

MOSES AND AL-KHIDR

Sura of the Cave

One day Moses said to his servant, I will not cease to go forward, until I come to the place where the two seas meet; or I will travel for a long space of time. But when they were arrived at the meeting of the two seas, they forgot their fish, which they had taken with them; and the fish took its way freely in the sea. And when they had passed beyond that place, Moses said unto his servant, Bring us our dinner; for now are we fatigued with this our journey. His servant answered, Dost thou know what has befallen me? When we took up our lodging at the rock, verily I forgot the fish: and none made me to forget it, except Satan, that I should not remind thee of it. And the fish took its way into the sea, in a wonderful manner. Moses said, This is what we sought after. And they both went back, returning by the way they came. And coming to the rock, they found one of our servants, unto whom we had granted mercy from us, and whom we had taught wisdom from before us. And Moses said unto him, Shall I follow thee, that thou mayest teach me part of that which thou hast been taught, for a direction unto me? He answered, Verily thou canst not bear with me: for how canst thou patiently suffer those things, the knowledge whereof thou dost not comprehend? Moses replied, Thou shalt find me patient, if God please; neither will I be disobedient unto thee in anything. He said, If thou follow me, therefore, ask me not concerning anything, until I shall declare the meaning thereof unto thee. So they went on by the sea-shore, until they went up into a ship; and he made a hole therein. And Moses said unto him, Hast thou made a hole therein, that thou mightest drown those who are on board? now hast thou done a strange thing. He answered, Did I not tell thee that thou couldest not bear with me? Moses said, Rebuke me not, because I did forget; and impose not on me a difficulty in what I am commanded. Wherefore they left the ship and proceeded, until they met with a youth, and he slew him. Moses said, Hast thou slain an innocent person, without his having killed another? now hast thou committed an unjust action. He answered, Did I not tell thee that thou couldest not bear with me? Moses said, If I ask thee concerning anything hereafter, suffer me not to accompany thee: now hast thou received an excuse from me. They went forwards, therefore, until they came to the inhabitants of a certain city: and they asked food of the inhabitants thereof; but they refused to receive them. And they found therein a wall, which was ready to fall down; and he set it upright. Whereupon Moses said unto him, If thou wouldest thou mightest doubtless have received a reward for it. He answered This shall be a separation between me and thee; but I will first declare unto thee the signification of that which thou couldest not bear with patience. The vessel belonged to certain poor men, who did their business in the sea: and I was minded to render it unserviceable, because there was a king behind them, who took every sound ship by force. As to the youth, his parents were true believers; and we feared, lest he, being an unbeliever, should oblige them to suffer his perverseness and ingratitude: wherefore we desired that their Lord might give them a more righteous child in exchange for him, and one more affectionate towards them. And the wall belonged to two orphan youths in the city, and under it was a treasure hidden which belonged to them; and their father was a righteous man: and thy Lord was pleased that they should attain their full age, and take forth their treasure, through the mercy of thy Lord, and I did not what thou hast seen of mine own will, but by God's direction. This is the interpretation of that which thou couldest not bear with patience. (xviii, 59–81)

MARY

Sura of Mary

And remember in the book of the Qur'ān the story of Mary, when she retired from her family to a place towards the east, and took a veil to conceal herself from them; and we sent our spirit Gabriel unto her, and he appeared unto her in the shape of a perfect man. She said, I fly for refuge unto the merciful God, that he may defend me from thee: if thou fearest him, thou wilt not approach me. He answered, Verily, I am the messenger of thy Lord, and am sent to give thee a holy son. She said, How shall I have a son, seeing a man hath not touched me, and I am no harlot? Gabriel replied, So shall it be: thy Lord saith, This is easy with me; and we will perform it, that we may ordain him for a sign unto men, and a mercy from us: for it is a thing which is decreed. Wherefore she conceived him; and she retired aside with him in her womb to a distant place; and the pains of child-birth came upon her near the trunk of a palm-tree. She said, Would to God I had died before this, and had become a thing forgotten and lost in oblivion. And he who was beneath her called to her, saying, Be not grieved; now hath God provided a rivulet under thee; and do thou shake the body of the palm-tree, and it shall let fall ripe dates upon thee ready gathered. And eat, and drink, and calm thy mind. Moreover, if thou see any man, and he question thee, say, Verily, I have vowed a fast unto the Merciful: wherefore I will by no means speak to a man this day. So she brought the child to her people, carrying him in her arms. And they said unto her, O

Mary, now hast thou done a strange thing. O sister of Aaron, thy father was not a bad man, neither was thy mother a harlot. But she made signs unto the child to answer them; and they said, How shall we speak to him, who is an infant in the cradle? Whereupon the child said, Verily I am the servant of God; he hath given me the book of the gospel, and hath appointed me a prophet. And he hath made me blessed, wheresoever I shall be; and hath commanded me to observe prayer, and to give alms, so long as I shall live; and he hath made me dutiful towards my mother, and hath not made me proud or unhappy. And peace be on me the day whereon I was born, and the day whereon I shall die, and the day whereon I shall be raised to life. This was Jesus, the son of Mary; the Word of truth, concerning whom they doubt. It is not meet for God, that he should have any son; God forbid! When he decreeth a thing, he only saith unto it, Be; and it is. And verily God is my Lord and your Lord; wherefore, serve him: this is the right way. Yet the sectaries differ among themselves concerning Jesus: but woe be unto those who are unbelievers, because of their appearance at the great day. Do thou cause them to hear, and do thou cause them to see, on the day whereon they shall come unto us to be judged: but the ungodly are this day in a manifest error. And do thou forewarn them of the day of sighing, when the matter shall be determined, while they are now sunk in negligence, and do not believe. Verily we will inherit the earth, and whatever creatures are therein; and unto us shall they all return. (xix, 16–41)

Mary under the palm tree. (Persian ms., B.N.)

JESUS

Sura of the Family of Imran*

The angels said, O Mary, verily God hath chosen thee, and hath purified thee, and hath chosen thee above all the women of the world: O Mary, be devout towards thy Lord, and worship, and bow down with those who bow down. This is a secret history: we reveal it unto thee, although thou wast not present with them when they threw in their rods to cast lots which of them should have the education of Mary; neither wast thou with them when they strove among themselves. When the angels said: O Mary, verily God sendeth thee good tidings, that thou shalt bear the Word proceeding from himself; his name shall be Christ Jesus the son of Mary, honourable in this world and in the world to come, and one of those who approach near to the presence of God; and he shall speak unto men in the cradle, and when he is grown up; and he shall be one of the righteous: she answered, Lord, how shall I have a son, since a man hath not touched me? the angel said, So God creatheth that which he pleaseth: when he decreeth a thing, he only saith unto it, Be, and it is: God shall teach him the scripture, and wisdom, and the law, and the gospel; and shall appoint him his apostle to the children of Israel; and he shall say, Verily I come unto you with a sign from your Lord; for I will make before you, of clay, as it were the figure of a bird; then I will breathe thereon, and it shall become a bird, by the permission of God; and I will heal him that hath been blind from his birth; and the leper; and I will raise the dead by the permission of God: and I will prophesy unto you what ye eat, and what ye lay up for store in your houses. Verily herein will be a sign unto you, if ye believe. And I come to confirm the law which was revealed before me, and to allow unto you as lawful part of that which hath been forbidden you: and I come unto you with a sign from your Lord; therefore fear God, and obey me. Verily God is my Lord, and your Lord; therefore serve him. This is the right way. But when Jesus perceived their

* 'Imrān is the name given to the father of Moses and Aaron and to the father of the Virgin Mary.

unbelief, he said, Who will be my helpers towards God? The apostles answered, We will be the helpers of God; we believe in God, and do thou bear witness that we are true believers. O Lord, we believe in that which thou hast sent down, and we have followed thy apostle; write us down therefore with those who bear witness of him. And the Jews devised a stratagem against him; but God devised a stratagem against them; and God is the best deviser of stratagems. When God said, O Jesus, verily I will cause thee to die, and I will take thee up unto me, and I will deliver thee from the unbelievers; and I will place those who follow thee above the unbelievers, until the day of resurrection: then unto me shall ye return, and I will judge between you of that concerning which ye disagree. Moreover, as for the infidels, I will punish them with a grievous punishment in this world, and in that which is to come; and there shall be none to help them. But they who believe, and do that which is right, he shall give them their reward: for God loveth not the wicked doers. These signs and this prudent admonition do we rehearse unto thee. Verily the likeness of Jesus in the sight of God is as the likeness of Adam; he created him out of the dust, and then said unto him, Be; and he was. This is the truth from thy Lord; be not therefore one of those who doubt; and whoever shall dispute with thee concerning him, after the knowledge which hath been given thee, say unto them, Come, let us call together our sons and your sons and our wives and your wives, and ourselves and yourselves; then let us make imprecations, and lay the curse of God on those who lie. Verily this is a true history: and there is no God but God; and God is most mighty and wise. If they turn back, God well knoweth the evil-doers. Say, O ye who have received the scripture, come to a just determination between us and you; that we worship not any except God, and associate no creature with him; and that the one of us take not the other for lords, beside God. But if they turn back, say, Bear witness that we are true believers. O ye to whom the scriptures have been given, why do ye dispute concerning Abraham, since the Law and the Gospel were not sent down until after him? Do ye not therefore understand? Behold ye are they who dispute concerning that which ye have some knowledge in; why therefore do you dispute concerning that which ye have no knowledge of? God knoweth, but ye know not. Abraham was neither a Jew nor a Christian; but he was of the true religion, one resigned unto God, and was not of the number of the idolaters. Verily the men who are the nearest of

kin unto Abraham are they who follow him: and this prophet, and they who believed on him: God is the patron of the faithful. Some of those who have received the scriptures desire to seduce you; but they seduce themselves only, and they perceive it not. O ye who have received the scriptures, why do ye not believe in the signs of God, since ye are witnesses of them? (iii, 37–63)

Muhammad disputing with the Christian bishop and the governor of Najran about Jesus. Miniature of the Arab school of Baghdad, dated 1217. It is the oldest known picture of Muhammad) (National Library, Cairo; recently discovered and published by Bishr Fares)

The Mystical Verses

Here are some of the Qur'ānic verses most frequently quoted by the mystics in an interior or esoteric (bāṭini) *sense; in these the Ṣūfis have found the core of their teaching.*

Ye were dead and he gave you life; He will hereafter cause you to die and will again restore you to life; then shall ye return unto Him. (ii, 26)

They shall meet their Lord, and to Him shall they return. (ii, 43)

We are God's and unto Him shall we surely return. (ii, 151)

His is the kingdom of the heaven and the earth, and unto God shall all things return. (lvii, 5)

It is to Him that ye shall return. (xxix, 20)

He createth and He restoreth to life; He is inclined to forgive and gracious; the possessor of the glorious throne. (lxxxv, 13–15)

Every soul shall taste death; then shall ye return to us. (xxix, 57)

Whithersoever ye turn yourselves to pray, there is the Face of God. (ii, 109)

Ye shall surely pass from state to state. (lxxxiv, 19)

God compasseth them around from every side. (lxxv, 20)

Everything shall perish except His face. (xxviii, 88)

Say: God! and leave them to their vain amusements. (vi, 91)

This present life is only a toy. (lvii, 19)

They make not a due estimation of God. (vi, 91)

Be mindful of Me, and I will be mindful of you. (ii, 147)

If ye love God, God shall love you. (iii, 29)

God knows, but ye do not know. (iii, 59)

I have chosen thee for Myself. (xx, 43)

Verily herein is an admonition unto him who hath a heart to understand, or giveth ear, and is present with an attentive mind. (1, 36)

O thou soul at rest, return unto thy Lord, well-pleased with Him, well-pleasing, unto Him. (lxxxix, 27f.)

A hermit visited by the emperor of India.
(India, 18th century)

*THE TRADITIONS**

True Islam

Chapter III—*A man is a true Muslim when no other Muslim has to fear anything from either his tongue or his hand.*

According to 'Abdallah ibn 'Amr the Prophet said 'A man is a true Muslim when no other Muslim has to fear anything from either his tongue or his hand. A man is a true Muhājir (Emigrant) when he flees from what God has forbidden to him.'

Chapter V—*Feeding (the hungry) belongs to Islam.*

'Abdallah ibn 'Amr records that a man once asked the Prophet what was the best thing in Islam, and the latter replied 'It is to feed (the hungry) and to give the greeting (of peace) both to those one knows and to those one does not know.'

Chapter VI—*To desire for one's neighbour what one desires for oneself is to perform an act of faith.*

According to Anas the Prophet said 'None of you really has faith unless he desires for his neighbour what he desires for himself.' Al-Ma'rūr said 'I met Abu Dharr at ar-Rābadhah. He was wearing a double garment and so was his servant. When I asked him about the similarity of their dress, he replied, "One day I insulted a man by saying disgraceful things about his mother. Thereupon the Prophet said to me 'Abu Dharr, you are insulting so-and-so with regard to his mother, so you are a man in whom there are still some pre-Islamic feelings. Those servants whom God has placed under your authority are your brothers. Anyone who is the master of his brother ought to give him to eat what he eats himself and to clothe him as he clothes himself. Do not burden your servants beyond their capacity, but if you happen to do so, go to help them'".'

---

* The author is indebted for these quotations to Bokhari's *Les Traditions Islamiques*. See Bibliography.

Prayer niche and pulpit in the mosque. Imam-Riza Meshhed

Anas ibn Mālik said, Abu Dharr recounted that the Messenger of God said, 'While I was at Mecca, the roof of my house opened and Gabriel entered. He opened my chest, washed me with the water of Zamzam, then brought a golden basin full of faith and wisdom and emptied all of it into my chest. After that he closed it, took me by the hand and raised me towards the lowest heaven. When I arrived at the lowest heaven, Gabriel said to the door-keeper "Open." "Who is there?" he asked. "Gabriel" the angel replied. "Is there anyone with you?" responded the door-keeper. "Yes" replied Gabriel, "Muḥammad is with me." "Has he been commanded?" added the door-keeper. "Yes," said the angel. When the door-keeper had opened to us, we rose up within the lowest heaven, and suddenly we saw a man sitting, having some spirits on his right and others on his left. Every time he looked to the right he smiled, but as soon as he looked to the left he wept. He said "Welcome virtuous prophet and virtuous son." "Who is this?" I asked of Gabriel. "This man", he replied "is Adam, and those spirits on his right and on his left are the souls of his descendants. Those on the right are destined to Paradise, while the spirits on his left are destined to Hell. That is why, when he looks to the right, he smiles, and when he looks to the left, he weeps."

'Then Gabriel raised me up to the second heaven and said to the door-keeper "Open." He asked the same questions as the first, and then opened to us.' Anas recounted that Abu Dharr said that the Prophet found in the various heavens Adam, Idris, Moses, Jesus and Abraham, but he was not certain which were the positions they occupied. What he does say is that Muḥammad found Adam in the lowest heaven and Abraham in the sixth heaven.

Anas adds 'When Gabriel came with the Prophet into the presence of Idris, the latter said "Welcome virtuous prophet."' 'When I asked "Who is this?"' the Prophet went on, 'Gabriel answered me "It is Idris". Then I went into the presence of Moses, who said "Welcome virtuous prophet and virtuous brother". "Who is this?" I asked. "Moses" replied the angel. I then went into the presence of Jesus, who exclaimed "Welcome virtuous prophet and virtuous brother". "Who is it?" I said. "Jesus" replied Gabriel. I went after that into the presence of Abraham, who said "Welcome virtuous prophet and virtuous brother". "Who is it?" I asked. "It is Abraham" the angel said to me.'

Ibn Ḥazm records that Ibn 'Abbās and Abu Habba al-Anṣāri said that the Prophet used the following words. 'Then the angel raised me until he brought me to a height where I heard the beating of wings.' Ibn Ḥazm and Anas ibn Mālik add the Prophet said 'Then God prescribed for my people fifty prayers (a day). As I came back with this regulation, I passed near Moses. "What has God prescribed for your people?" he asked. "He has prescribed fifty prayers" I replied. "Go back to the Lord" said Moses, "for your people will not be strong enough to endure that. So I went

The Prophet, mounted on the mare Buraq, passes through the celestial spheres

back into the presence of God, who reduced the number by half. Then when I came near Moses, I said to him "They have been reduced by half". "Go back to the Lord" he said, "for your people will not be strong enough to endure that." I went back into the presence of God, who reduced the number again by half. Coming back to Moses, I told him of this new reduction. "Go back to the Lord" he replied, "for your people will not have the strength to endure that". I went back into the presence of God and he said to me "There will be five prayers then, but they will be worth fifty in my eyes, for nothing can be changed of what has been spoken in my presence" I went back to Moses, who said to me again "Go back to the Lord". "I am ashamed before the Lord" I replied. Then Gabriel led me away and brought me to the lote-tree of the Boundary, which is covered with unspeakably beautiful colours. Next I entered Paradise. There are domes of pearls and the sun there is made of musk.'

The Prophet is received in heaven by the angels who are still separated from the divine glory by 70,000 *curtains of light, of darkness and of fire.*
(*Book of the Assumption, Turkish ms., B.N.*)

The Unalterable Religion

Abu Salāmah ibn 'Abd ar-Raḥmān was informed that Abu Hurairah said 'The Messenger of God spoke thus. "There is no new born child but belongs (naturally) to the religion of Islam. It is the parents who make it a Jew or a Christian or a Magian. Similarly every animal is born complete. Have you ever seen one come into the world with its ears cut?"' Then Abu Hurairah recited the verses of the Qur'ān 'Turn towards the natural religion in which God created men. God's creation cannot be changed. That is the unalterable religion.' (Sura xxx, verse 29)

The True Fast

Of those who do not give up speaking lies and practising deception during the fast the Prophet, according to Abu Hurairah, said 'If anyone does not give up speaking lies and practising deception, God is not concerned with his abstaining from drinking and eating'.

Good done to Animals

According to Abu Hurairah, the Messenger of God said 'A man travelling along a road felt extremely thirsty and went down a well and drank. When he came up he saw a dog panting with thirst and licking the (moist) earth. "This animal" the man said "is suffering from thirst just as much as I was". So he went down the well again, filled his shoe with water, and taking it in his teeth climbed out of the well and gave the water to the dog. God was pleased with his act and granted him pardon (for his sins).'

Someone said 'O Messenger of God, will we then have a reward for (the good done to) our animals?' 'There will be a reward' he replied 'for anyone who gives water to a being that has a tender heart.'

According to Asmā' bint Abu Bakr, the Prophet, after having completed the prayer during an eclipse, said 'Hell fire came near me until I cried out "Lord, am I to be one of them?"' Then the

Prophet saw a woman—'And I think' said Asmā' 'that he added "whom a cat was scratching" '—and said 'What does this mean?' 'This woman' the reply came 'shut up this cat and allowed it to die of hunger.'

According to 'Abdallah ibn 'Umar, the Messenger of God said 'A woman was cruel to a cat by shutting it up and allowing it to die of hunger. Because of that, this woman went to Hell.' And he added 'if I mistake not, God said to her "You did not give it anything to eat or drink when you shut it up, and you did not give it freedom to go in search of prey from which to live".'

When the Messenger of God was asked about asses, he replied 'There has been no special revelation about them, however in their general sense these verses alone are applicable to them "Whoever does good will see it even if it is only the weight of a grain, and whoever does evil will see it even if it is only the weight of a grain".' (Sura xcix, verses 7 and 8)

Paradise in the Shadow of Sabres

Abu Mūsā said 'A man came to find the Prophet and said to him "Some men fight for booty, others for glory, others out of ostentation, but who is really in the way of God?' The Prophet answered "If a man fights in order that the word of God may be above everything, he is in the way of God".' Anas ibn Mālik said the Prophet said 'None of the elect of Paradise would be willing to come back to this world, no matter which wordly treasures he was to possess, with the exception of martyrdom. For it he would wish to come back to this world and be killed again ten times even, because of what he knows of heavenly favours.'

Paradise is under flashing sabres. Al-Mughīrah ibn Shu'bah said 'A prophet has taught us, following what he learned from our Lord, that if any of us is killed, he will enter Paradise.' 'Umar said to the Prophet 'Are our dead in Paradise and theirs in Hell?' 'Undoubtedly' replied the Prophet. Sālim Abu-'n-Naḍr, a freedman of 'Umar ibn 'Ubaid Allah, who also acted as his secretary, said that 'Abdallah ibn Abu 'Awfā wrote to the latter that the Messenger of God had said 'Know that Paradise is under the shadow of swords.' About the man who wants to have a son for the Holy War, according to Abu Hurairah, the Messenger of God said ‘Solomon, son of David, once said, “This night I want to have intercourse with a hundred women, one after another—or with ninety-nine—so that each of them will give birth to a warrior who will fight in the way of God”. “Add ‘If God will’” said his friend to him, but Solomon did not say it, and only one of his wives became pregnant, and she gave birth to the half of a child. By him in whose hands Muḥammad is, if he had said “If God will” (Solomon would have had from all his wives) warriors who would all have fought in the way of God.’

Solomon and the Queen of Sheba.
(16th century Persian ms., B.N.)

Khadījah

The marriage of the Prophet with Khadījah and the merits of this lady.

With various *isnāds* [chains of authorities] 'Abdallah ibn Ja'far records that he heard 'Ali ibn Abu Ṭālib say that he had heard the Prophet remark 'The best of women (in the world) was Mary. The best of women [of this people] was Khadījah.

Al-Laith reported that Hishām, who had it from his father, had written to him that 'Ā'ishah said 'I was never jealous of any of the wives of the Prophet as I was of Khadījah, although she was dead before I became the Prophet's wife, because I often heard him speak of her, since God had commanded him to tell her that she would have [in Paradise] a house of pearls, and also because, when he killed a sheep, he sent a large part to the friends of Khadījah.'

According to 'Urwa, 'Ā'ishah said Hāla Bint Khuwailid, the sister of Khadījah, asked to be admitted to the presence of the Messenger of God, and the latter, recognizing Khadījah's manner, was upset and exclaimed "By God, it is Hāla." Stung by jealousy, I said to the Prophet "Why do you revive the memory of these old women of Quraish with red gums [toothless], who are victims of age? God has now given you something better in place of them".'

Justice

According to Anas ibn Mālik, the Prophet said 'Help your brother whether he is oppressor or oppressed.'

According to Anas, after the Messenger of God said 'Help your brother whether he is oppressor or oppressed', Anas replied to him 'O Messenger of God, a man who is oppressed I am ready to help, but how does one help an oppressor?' 'By hindering him doing wrong' he said.

According to 'Abdallah ibn 'Umar, the Prophet said 'Injustice will make darkness on the day of resurrection.'

According to Ibn 'Abbās, the Prophet sent Mu'ādh to the Yemen saying 'Fear the curse of the oppressed, for there is no veil between it and God.'

Married to the wealthy Khadijah (top left), Muhammad (on a camel) is able, thanks to her, to give up his occupation of caravaneer and devote himself to his mission

The Martyrdom of Khubaid

Abu Hurairah said: The Prophet had sent out a reconnoitring detachment under the leadership of 'Āṣim ibn Thābit, the grandfather of 'Āṣim ibn 'Umar ibn al-Khaṭṭāb. They had come to a place between 'Usfān and Mecca, when they got word of a tribe of the Hudhail called the Banu Liḥyān. About a hundred archers followed their route and, when they reached one of the encampments they had occupied, found the kernels of dates which they had received as provisions at Medina. 'These kernels,' they said, 'come from the dates of Yathrib.' They continued their pursuit and overtook them. 'Āṣim and his companions then withdrew to (the hill of) Fadfad, where they were observed by the Banu Liḥyān. 'If you come down to us,' said the Banu Liḥyān, 'we promise formally not to put one of you to death.' 'For myself,' replied 'Āṣim, 'I would not come down to put myself at the mercy of an infidel. O my God, inform thy Prophet of our situation.' 'Āṣim and six of his companions were killed by arrows, so that there remained only Khubaid, Zaid and one other individual. These were promised safe conduct and, when they had received this, came down from their place of refuge. The Banu Liḥyān seized the three men and, taking the strings from their bows, bound them. 'There is the first treachery,' cried the third individual; and he refused to follow the men. At first they dragged him, then they tried to make him get up; but, as he did nothing, they killed him. Then they led away Khubaid and Zaid, and sold them at Mecca. The family of al-Ḥārith ibn 'Āmir ibn Nawfal bought Khubaid, who had killed al-Ḥārith at the battle of Badr. They held him prisoner for some time and resolved to put him to death.

Khubaid had asked one of the daughters of al-Ḥārith for a razor to shave his pubis. This woman described how, after lending him this razor, she one day failed to keep a close watch on her child, and the latter went to Khubaid, who took him on his lap. As Khubaid had a razor in his hand the young woman was greatly afraid. 'Would you be afraid,' said Khubaid, 'that I might kill your child; it is a thing that, please God, I shall never do.' 'Never,' said the young woman, 'have I seen a prisoner as good as Khubaid; one day I saw him eat a fresh grape when there was no such fruit in Mecca and he was closely bound; it must have been God who satisfied him with such a favour.'

As they led him away to kill him outside the sacred territory,

Khubaid said: 'Let me make a prayer of two rak'as.' When he had completed this he turned to his executioners and said: 'If I had not been afraid that you thought that I was afraid of death, I should have prayed more.' It was he who set the example of the prayer of two rak'as before enduring death. At last he said again: 'O my God, count how many they are,' and he recited this verse:

From the time I became a Muslim, it did not matter from which side I should be killed, since it is for God that I die.

He is the Supreme Being who has decided thus; His blessing will enable my dismembered limbs to reassemble again.

'Uqbah ibn al-Ḥārīth then killed Khubaib. The Quraish despatched some men to 'Āṣim's corpse, in order to bring him a part of the body which would enable them to confirm his identity, because 'Āṣim had killed one of their chief people at the battle of Badr. But God had sent a veritable cloud of wasps to protect the body from dishonourable treatment, and the messengers returned without bringing the least thing.

Hospitality

On the words of the Qur'ān: '. . . and they prefer the others before themselves, although there be indigence among them'. (lix, 9)

According to Abu Hurairah, a man came to find the Prophet and the latter asked his wives for something to give him to eat. 'We have absolutely nothing,' they replied, 'except water.' 'Who wants to share his meal with this man?' asked the Prophet; or, according to a variant, 'who wants to give him hospitality?' A man of the Anṣār then said, 'I'. Then he led this man to his wife and said to her: 'Treat generously the guest of the Messenger of God.' She replied: 'We have nothing except our children's supper.' 'Oh, well,' he replied, 'get your meal ready, light your lamp, and when your children want supper, put them to bed.' So the woman prepared the meal, lit the lamp, put the children to bed, then, getting up as if to trim the lamp, she extinguished it. The Anṣāri and his wife then made as if to eat, but in fact they spent the night with empty stomachs. The next day when the Anṣāri went to find the Messenger of God, the latter said to him: 'This night God smiled', or, according to a variant, 'God has admired the way you acted'. It was then that God revealed these words [of the Qur'ān]: 'and they prefer the others before themselves, although there be indigence among them.'

Magnanimity

Jābir ibn 'Abdallāh told Sinān ibn Abi-Sinān ad-Du'ali that he once made an expedition in the direction of Nejd with the Messenger of God. When they were returning, the great heat of midday came upon them when they were in a valley abounding with acacias. The Messenger of God went and rested under a mimosa tree, hanging his sword on it. 'We had had a sleep,' added Jābir, 'when the Messenger of God called us.' We ran to him and saw a bedouin seated beside him. 'This bedouin,' said the Prophet, 'drew my sword from its sheath while I slept; then I awoke and saw him with my sword naked in his hand. "Who shall defend you against me?" he said. "God," I replied. Now this bedouin is once more seated.' The Messenger of God did not inflict any punishment on him.

The Laws of War

Of the mission given by the Prophet to Khālid ibn al-Walīd against the Banū Judhaimah.

'Abdallāh ibn 'Umar said: 'The Prophet sent Khālid ibn al-Walid to the Banū Judhaimah. Summoned by Khālid to embrace Islam, the Banū Judhaimah, instead of using the good formula (*aslamnā*), said: *saba'nā, saba'nā.* Khālid then set about killing and taking prisoners in the tribe, and he handed over each prisoner

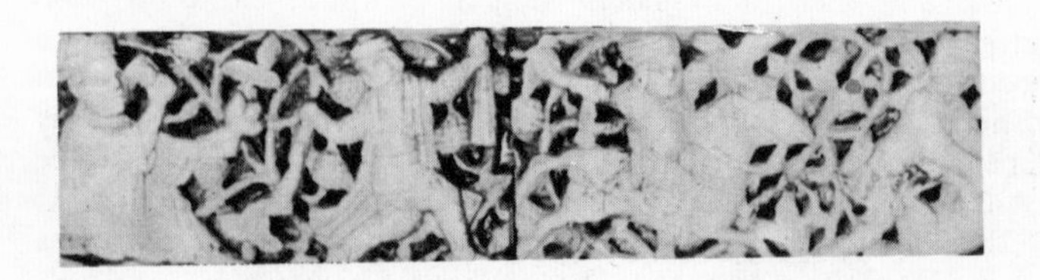

he had made to one of us. Then one day he ordered each of us to kill our prisoner. "I will not kill my prisoner," I then said, "and none of my companions will kill his." When we returned to the Prophet, we told him about this. He at once raised his hand and exclaimed, "O my God, I am innocent before thee of the act committed by Khālid." '

The Humble and the Gentle

Ḥārithah ibn Wahb al-Khuzā'i tells how he heard the Prophet say: 'Have I not taught you how the inhabitants of Paradise will be all the humble and the weak, whose oaths God will accept when they swear to be faithful? Have I not taught you how the inhabitants of Hell will be all the cruel beings, strong of body and arrogant?'

An expedition of the Companions of the Prophet, as depicted by a miniaturist from Turkestan in the 14th century.
(Royal Asiatic Society)

According to Anas the Prophet said: 'At the Judgement Day the believers will assemble and will say: "Let us ask someone to intercede for us." They will go and find Adam and say to him: "You are the father of mankind; God has created you with His hand, He has taught the angels to kneel before you, and He has taught you the names of all things. Intercede to the Lord on our

Hell.
The Prophet and Gabriel see the damned fixed to hooks over a fire guarded by a demon.
(*Book of the Assumption, Turkish ms., B.N.*)

behalf in order that He may deliver us from our present predicament." He will reply: "I am not the one you are needing. Go and find Noah; he is the first messenger whom God sent to mankind." They will find Noah, and he will say: "I am not the one you need." He will remind them that he asked the Lord about things of which he could have no knowledge, and he would be ashamed to intercede for them. "Go," he will say to them, "and find the Friend of the Merciful" [*sc*. Abraham]. They will do as they are bid, and the latter will say: "Go and ask Moses, this worshipper to whom God has addressed a word and to whom He has given the Torah [Pentateuch]." They will go and find Moses, and he will say to them: "I am not he whom you need." He will tell them that he killed a man who was not guilty, and that he is ashamed before his Lord. Then he arranges for them to approach Jesus, the worshipper of God and His messenger, the Word of God and the Spirit of God. But Jesus will say to them: "I am not he whom you need; go and find Muḥammad (God bless and preserve him!) he is the servant for whom God has pardoned all faults, past and future." Then they will come to me; I shall go to the Lord and ask Him if He will listen to me. He will grant me my request, and when I see him, I shall fall down on my knees and remain there as long as it pleases Him. Then He will say to me: "Look up; ask and you shall receive; speak and you will be heard; intercede and your intercession will be granted." Then I shall raise my head; I shall praise the Lord, following the formula which He will teach me; then I shall intercede. The Eternal One will show me a group of people, for whom I shall gain access into Paradise. This done, I shall return again to the Lord, and when I have seen Him, under the same condition as before, I shall intercede afresh. He will show me a second group, for whom I shall gain access to Paradise. Then I shall do the same a third and a fourth time, and shall say: "There are no more for Hell except those whom the Qur'ān has condemned to it, and who must live in it for ever." '

A Mystical Dowry

Chapter XXII—*On repeating the Qur'ān from memory.*

According to Sahl ibn Sa'd, a woman came and found the Messenger of God and said to him: 'O Messenger of God, I have come to offer you my person.' The Messenger of God turned and regarded her. Then, having looked at her hard, he lowered his head. The woman, seeing that he did not make any decision about her, sat down. Then one of the Companions of the Prophet got

up and said: 'O Messenger of God, if you do not need her, let me marry her.' 'Have you any possessions,' asked the Prophet. 'No, by God, O Messenger of God.' 'Then go home and see if you can find something.' The man went away, then came back and said: 'By God, O Messenger of God, I have found nothing.' 'See if you could not find a simple iron ring.' The man went away, then came back and said: 'No, by God, O Messenger of God, I have not even an iron ring, but here is my *izār* [waist-wrapper].' Sahl added that he had not a garment of which he could have given her the half. 'What good would your izār be?' asked the Messenger

The bride's procession.
(*Mesopotamia*, 1237; *B.N.*)

of God; 'if you wear it, it will be of no use to her, and if she wears it, you will have nothing on you'. The man sat down, remained for a long time on the same spot, then got up to go. When the Messenger of God saw him disappearing, he ordered him to be called back, and when the man had returned, he said to him: 'What do you know of the Qur'ān?' 'I know such-and-such a sura and such-and-such a sura'; and he made a list of them. 'You know them by heart?' 'Yes.' 'Then go, I give you this woman since you know the Qur'ān.'

Consent to Marriage

Chapter XLII—*Neither the father nor anyone else can give a woman in marriage without her consent, whether she is a virgin or has already been married.*

Abu Ḥurairah reported that the Prophet said: 'the woman who has already been married can only be given in marriage by her own order; the virgin cannot be given in marriage until her consent has been asked.' 'And how will she give her consent, O Messenger of God?' asked the faithful. 'By keeping silence,' replied the Prophet. Abu 'Amr, the freedman of 'Ā'ishah, reports that the latter said: 'a virgin has shame.' 'Her consent,' he replied, 'is indicated by silence.'

To Straighten a Rib

Chapter LXXX—*Advice in respect of women.*

According to Abu Ḥurairah the Prophet said: 'Let him who believes in God and in the Day of Judgement not harm his neighbour; enjoin him to treat women well. They were created from a rib, and in a rib it is the highest part which is most bent. If you try to straighten it, you break it. If you leave it, it remains bent. Exhort them, then, to be good to women.'

Ibn 'Umar said: 'During the Prophet's lifetime we avoided talking or joking with our wives, lest we should draw some revelation upon ourselves. But when the Prophet had died, we talked and joked with them.'

Duties and Rights

Chapter LXXXIX—'*Your wife has rights over you,' said the Prophet, according to Abū Juhaifa.*

'Abdallāh ibn 'Amr ibn al-'Ās tells how the Messenger of God said to him: 'O 'Abdallāh, is it good for you that, so they tell me, you fast by day and again by night?' 'O Messenger of God,' I replied, 'it is true.' 'Then do not act thus,' he replied: 'fast and break the fast (by turns); get up (for prayer) and then sleep. You have a duty towards your body, your eyes have rights over you, and your wife has rights over you.'

The Forty Ḥadīth

Here are some of the well-known Forty Ḥadīth chosen by Nawāji (from the translation by G. H. Bousquet, *Les Classiques de l'Islam*, 1950).

According to Abu Dharr (may God be pleased with him!) some Companions of the Messenger of God (God bless and preserve him!) said to him: 'O Messenger of God, the richest people have monopolized the rewards. They pray like us, fast like us, and, what is more, they give alms out of the surplus of their wealth.' 'What?' he replied, 'has God given you nothing from which to give alms? To say "Glory be to God!" is an alms, "God is great" is also an alms, and likewise "Praise be to God! there is no other god but God." Each time you command good to be done it is an alms; and each time you refrain from evil it is an alms. Each time you have sexual intercourse it is an alms.'

Upon this they exclaimed, 'What? each of us could satisfy his fleshly appetites and would gain a reward thereby?' He replied: 'Look, he who satisfies his appetites in an unlawful manner, is he not committing a sin? In the same way he who satisfies them lawfully, the same shall receive a reward.'

Wābisah ibn Ma'bad (may God be pleased with him!) said: 'I went to see the Messenger of God (God bless and preserve him!) and he said to me: 'You want to question me on the subject of virtue?'

'Yes,' I replied, and he went on: 'Question your heart. Virtue is that by which the soul enjoys repose and the heart tranquillity. Sin is what introduces trouble into the soul and tumult into man's bosom—and this despite the religious advice which men may give you.'

According to Abu Sa'īd Sa'd ibn Mālik ibn Sinān al-Khudri (may God be pleased with him!) the Messenger of God (God bless and preserve him!) said: 'Do no evil, and do not return evil for evil.'

Incense-burner (Yemen)

A SURVEY OF JURISPRUDENCE

IBN KHALDŪN*

The Sources of Islamic Law

The Four Sources of Fiqh

One of the greatest of the religious sciences and one of the most important and most useful has for its object the bases of jurisprudence. It consists in examining the statements which occur in the sacred texts in order to distinguish the maxims (of law) and the obligatory duties (of religion). The principles contained in the law are founded on the Book, that is the Qur'ān, then on the Sunnah, which is used to explain the Book. While the Prophet was alive, judgements (or legal maxims) were obtained directly from him. He elucidated by his words and deeds the matter of the Qur'ān which God had revealed to him, and gave oral instruction to his followers. Thus they had no need to have recourse to tradition, speculation or analogical deduction. This oral instruction came to an end at the death of the Prophet, and thereafter the knowledge of what was prescribed by the Qur'ān was conserved only by tradition.

---

* *Muqaddima*, French translation of de Slane, 1868 (1938), Vol. III, p. 25. Ibn Khaldūn, 1332–1406, was the last of the great thinkers of mediaeval Islam and a forerunner of sociology and the philosophy of history.

The mosque at Kairouan

Let us pass to the Sunnah. The Companions all agreed to recognize that for Muslims it was a duty to conform to the prescriptions contained in the Sunnah and founded on the words and deeds of the Prophet, provided that these statements were handed down by a tradition that was sufficiently sound to give complete conviction of their authenticity. That is why the Qur'ān and the Sunnah are regarded as the sources from which must be drawn the assertions which lead to the solution of legal questions. Later, the general consensus (of the first Muslims on certain points of law) took its place (as authority) by the side of these two (sources of doctrine; this consensus existed) because the Companions showed themselves unanimous in rejecting the opinions of any individual who did not share their view. This unanimity must have rested on a solid basis, for the consensus of such men as these was certainly founded on good reasons. Besides, we have sufficient proofs to know that the feeling of the (Muslim) community could not go astray. The general consensus was thus recognized as an authentic basis of proof in questions connected with the law.

If we examine the procedures by which the Companions and the earliest Muslims deduced from the Qur'ān and the Sunnah (legal maxims), we see that in bringing together analogous cases and comparing a doubtful case with others resembling it, they sacrificed their personal opinions to the necessity of unanimity. Let us explain. After the death of the Prophet, many cases cropped up whose solution could not be found in the authentic texts (the Qur'ān and the Sunna). The Companions thereupon set themselves to judge these cases by comparing them with analogous cases whose solution was already known, and in relating them to the texts which had been used to settle these other cases. In this process of comparison they were careful to observe certain rules by means of which the analogy of the two similar, or somewhat similar, cases could be strictly determined. In this way they reached the conviction that the divinely given decision in one of these cases applied equally to the other. This operation, which they all agreed to regard as furnishing a legal proof, was called Qiyās (analogical deduction) and forms the fourth source of principles.

These then, according to the great majority of scholars, are the sources to which one has recourse in order to settle legal questions. Some jurists, however, though admittedly only a few, differ from this view in respect of general consensus and analogical deduction. There are also certain scholars who to these four sources add a fifth, of which it is not necessary to speak, since its applications are not important and its adherents are few.*

ABU SHUJĀ'†

The Five Pillars According to the 'Mukhtaṣar'

The five fundamental religious duties.—There are five prayers which are canonically obligatory: (1) the midday prayer. The first moment (at which it can take place) is when the sun (begins to) decline. The last moment is when each object has a shadow of a length equal to its own, not including the length of the shadow (at the moment of the sun's beginning) to decline. (2) The afternoon prayer. The first moment for it is when the shadow is greater than the object (not including the shadow at the moment of the sun's beginning to decline). The last moment for it is preferably the moment when the shadow is double the object (not including the shadow at the moment of the sun's beginning to decline), but it is permissible to delay it until the sun disappears. (3) The sunset prayer. For this there is but a single moment, namely, when the sun has disappeared. (4) The evening prayer. Its first moment is marked by the disappearance of the last red in the evening sky; as to its end, it is preferable that it should coincide with the first third of the night, but it is permissible to delay it until the rising of the second dawn. (5) The morning prayer. Its first moment is marked by the rising of the second dawn; and its end should preferably coincide with (the moment when) the dawn breaks over all the sky, but it is permissible to delay it until sunrise.

The conditions which make the prayer canonically obligatory are three: being a Muslim, having reached puberty, being in possession of one's reason. Five prayers are traditionally recommended: those of the two feasts (*'Īd al-Kabīr*; *'Īd as-Ṣaghīr*), those of the eclipses of the moon and sun, and that (for rain) in times of drought.

---

* The reference is doubtless to the Ṣūfis.

† G. H. Bousquet, *Le droit musulman par les textes*, Paris 1940, 114–118.

The *Zakāt* (or legal tithe, or legal alms) is obligatorily (payable) on five things: herds, grain, fruit, precious metals, merchandise. As to animals, the zakāt is obligatorily levied on three kinds: the camel species, the bovine species, and the smaller pastoral animals (sheep and goats). There are six conditions which make the payment of the zakāt for them obligatory, namely: being a Muslim, being free, having full ownership, having more than the minimum liable to zakāt, having possession throughout the year, having actually put the animals to pasture. As for precious metals, zakāt is levied on two things, gold and silver, and there are five conditions which make it obligatory: being a Muslim, being free, having full ownership, having more than the minimum, having possession throughout the year. As for grain, zakāt is obligatory on three conditions: it concerns plants sown in order to be used for food, and which have been set aside as such, and which are more than the taxable minimum, say, five *wasq* or bushels without the husks. As for fruits, zakāt is obligatory on those produced by date-palms and vines subject to the fulfilment of four conditions: being a Muslim, being free, having full ownership, having more than the minimum. As for merchandise, the conditions which make the zakāt obligatory are those which apply to precious metals.

Three elements (really four) constitute the conditions making the fast (*ṣawm*) obligatory: being a Muslim, having reached puberty, having one's reason, having the physical capacity (to accomplish it). The precepts of the fast, canonically obligatory, are five in number: the intention, abstinence from food, from drink, from sexual intercourse and from voluntary vomiting. There are ten things by which the fast may be broken: what one voluntarily causes to enter the stomach or the head; anything injected into the two openings (the anus and the urethra); voluntary vomiting; voluntary vaginal copulation; any other spermatic flow after masturbation; menstruation; the lochia; insanity; apostasy.

Three rules are 'recommended' with regard to the fast: the prompt breaking of it, the slow consumption of the meal taken before dawn, the renunciation of indecent gossip. . . .

Seven things make the pilgrimage (*ḥajj*) obligatory: being a Muslim, having reached puberty, having one's reason, being free, being able to find a mount and provisions, the route being safe, being able to complete the journey. The fundamental elements of the pilgrimage are four in number; sacralization (adoption of the state of iḥrām or taboo), together with the intention to perform the pilgrimage; the standing at 'Arafāt; the circumambulation of the House (the Ka'ba); the running between al-Ṣafā and al-Marwah. As to the fundamental elements of the '*umrah* (or lesser pilgrimage), they are three in number: the wearing of the iḥrām at certain times and places; the stoning of three heaps of stones; the shaving (of one's hair). The practices connected with the pilgrimage which are traditionally 'recommended' are seven in number: the ifrād or performance of the *ḥajj* before the '*umrah*; the use of the formula '*labbaika*' (Here am I, O God!) the circumambulation (of the Ka'bah) on arrival; the spending of the night at Muzdalifah; the two rak'as at the circumambulation; the spending of the night at Minā; the farewell circumambulation. In the state of iḥrām one must not wear any sewn clothing, but only the white *izār* (waist-wrapper) and the white *ridā'* (cloak).

The pilgrims, in the costume of ihram and with bare heads, proceeding from 'Arafat to Mina. (Photo by Jean Roman)

'In the name of God, the Merciful, the Compassionate.' (Usual formula at the beginning of religious acts)

Tolerance and 'open' religion

'No constraint in religion.' (Qur'ān, ii, 257) *This decisive divine word sets forth the principle of tolerance, which is generally followed, though not always perfectly. It makes itself heard above the numerous appeals to arms in defence of a country seriously threatened which from time to time during the first ten years of the Hijrah stimulated the ardour of the Arabs, both cultivators and bedouin, who in general, whatever we may think, were little enough inclined to sustained warlike effort. In the conquered countries the People of the Book, Jews and Christians, had to be not only tolerated but by statutory right protected and to have their religion respected. The poll-tax which they paid took the place of military service. Muḥammad's idea was that fundamentally all the prophets had proclaimed the same religion; if divergences showed themselves, this could only be because of ill-will, falsification or deformation; he, as the Seal of the Prophets, had come to fulfil, correct and give the perfect form to this revealed religion which had its beginnings in Abraham. In our time the reformer Muḥammad 'Abduh writes:* 'The Bible, the New Testament and the Qur'ān are three concordant books; religious men study all three and respect them equally. Thus the divine teaching is completed, and the true religion shines across the centuries.'

In principle, idolaters, polytheists and peoples devoid of all revelation had, so to speak, no rights. The point was debated in the cases of the Zoroastrians or Parsees and the Hindus, since it was clearly not possible to exterminate them. The view seems to have prevailed that they also had authorized Books, however mutilated or badly understood they might be. We know that the emperor Akbar, one of the

Muslim and Hindu ascetics mixing fraternally. (The age of Akbar dreamed of this reconciliation)

great rulers and great spirits of history, managed—clearly to his advantage—to reconcile and syncretize Islam and Hinduism.

It goes without saying that the rigidly '*closed*' *religion of the fuqahā' and of the masses readily damns all unbelievers. It is chiefly among the philosophers and the Ṣūfis that one finds a completely* '*open*' *conception of religion and of man's condition. For the former all intelligence necessarily has a share in the Active Intellect. For the latter what matters is their interior religion, the yearnings of the purified heart, the generosity of the spirit, and the force of the love encompassing all beings.*

The Qur'ān had also spoken against all racialism, and had commanded justice in international relations, and moderation even in times of war.

'O men, show great and scrupulous regard for your Master, who created you from a single being, then from this being drew his helpmate, and from this couple all the multitude of men and women which make up mankind' (iv, 1).

'O men, We have created you from a man and from a woman. We have divided you into peoples and tribes so that you might recognize each other' (xlix, 13). *Each sect and each party is* 'content with what it has' (xxx, 31), *said God, not without a certain irony in respect of conceited and childish pretensions.* 'If God had so wanted, He could have made of you a single people. . . . Strive with one another to perform good deeds. Ye all will return to God; He Himself will make clear to you that about which ye dispute' (v, 53). *The Ḥadīth proclaim that there is no essential difference between the races of mankind, that God has sent His mercy* 'to the red and to the black', *and that* 'an Arab is not superior to a foreigner or a white man to a black man except in his piety.' *Someone once called Bilāl the Abyssinian* 'the son of a negress'; *and the Prophet reprimanded him for having shown* 'pre-Islamic sentiments'.

Certain of the first Ṣūfis, like Bistāmi and Tustari, envisaged without daring to say so, universal salvation, the final extinction of Hell, and the conversion of Iblis.

The great Persian poets never ceased to insist on the relativity of the faiths in comparison with Reality and Love.

Ḥallāj said (Diwān, *ed. Massignon, 1931, 84*):

'I have reflected on the particular religions and tried to understand them, and I have come to regard them as a single principle with numerous ramifications. Therefore do not ask a man to adopt this or that particular religion, for that would lead him away from the fundamental Principle.

'It is this Principle itself which must go and look for him, this Principle in which all greatnesses and all meanings become clear; and Man, then, will understand.'

In the Mathnāvi *Jalāl ad-Dīn ar-Rūmi tells the following apologue:*

'A Persian, a Turk, a Byzantine and an Arab received a dirham and began to argue about the use to which they would put this money. One wanted to buy some angur, another some uzum, another some estafil (staphylos), and the last 'inab. Eventually they noticed that all four wanted grapes.'

The same idea is to be found in Sanā'i:

'Some blind men met an elephant, and each one groping felt one of its limbs. This animal has the shape of a carpet, said one touching its ear. No, a pipe, declared another, touching its trunk. Of a pillar, insisted one who felt its leg. Thus the majority of men only see a part of the universe, and their spirit is peopled with phantoms.'

'God knows, and ye know not,' *says the Qur'ān* (*ii, 213*).

In a poem Ibn 'Arabi, the Interpreter of the Desires, says:

'My heart is capable of all forms. It is a pasture for the gazelles, a convent for the Christian monks, a temple for idols, the Ka'bah of the pilgrims, the Tables of the Mosaic Law and the Book of the Qur'ān.

'I am, for myself, the religion of love. Whichever way the camel of love may take, my religion and my faith are there.'

Encouraged by kings like Akbar, the poets of the Indian empire pushed syncretism to the extreme, at a time when the Sufis were having friendly discussions with the yogis and competing with them.

Abu-'l-Faḍl (*Fazl*) *wrote in his* Akbar-Nameh (*Blochmann*, 'Ain-i-Akbari, *xxxiii*):

'One day I visit the church, another day the mosque; but from one temple to another I seek only Thee.

'For Thy students there is neither heresy nor orthodoxy; all see Thy truth without veils.

'Let the heretic keep his heresy and the orthodox his orthodoxy; Thy faithful one is the Merchant of Perfumes; he needs the essence of the rose of the divine love.'

The great Ṣūfi masters and the thinkers of Islam have not gone so far. They have held that it was necessary to respect strictly the external Law in order to follow the interior Way, since esotericism and exotericism complement each other without contradiction. Yet, even so, they have 'opened' in the Bergsonian sense, not only the gates of ijtihād (*intellectual effort in interpretation*), *but also those of religion. Their worship is no more social and communal but universal, because it is truly intellectual and proceeds from the heart. Has not God said in a famous verse* (*Qur'ān xxxiii, 72*), *which affirms both the grandeur and the moral liberty of man:*

'We proposed the faith unto the heavens and the earth and the mountains, and they refused to undertake the same, and were afraid thereof; but man undertook it; verily he became unjust and foolish.'

What was 'proposed', said Averroes, was the 'true interpretation'.

'The universe cannot contain Me,' *says a 'sacred'* (qudsi) *ḥadīth* (*one in which the Prophet reports God's speech to him*), 'but the heart of the believer contains Me.'

Ghazāli and interior religion

Abu Ḥāmid al-Ghazāli, who was born at Tus in Khurāsān in 450/1058 and died in the same town in 505/1111, at the age of twenty passed through an intellectual crisis which made him doubt the foundations of all knowledge. Later, as professor at Baghdad, he wrote the Tahāfut al-Falāsifah *against the Aristotelian* (*or Neoplatonic*) *philosophers. A new crisis made him leave his chair to practise asceticism and Ṣūfism. He then wrote the* Iḥyā' 'Ulūm ad-Dīn *to* 'revive the sciences of religion', *to show that juridical science with its formal rules, though useful for social practice, is insufficient in the spiritual life, and to reconcile Law and Reality, the exoteric and the esoteric. On taking up teaching again at Nishāpur, he wrote the* Munqidh, *in which he sketches his philosophical and spiritual journey, and passes beyond scholasticism and canon law to achieve a conquest of Knowledge and Love by the purification of hearts.*

Here are some pages from the Chapter on the Love of God (maḥabbah *in the* hyā', *following the unpublished French translation of G. Laurès from the Cairo edition of 1358/1939, Vol. iv*).

Bismillah ar-Rahman ar-Rahim.
(*In the name of God, the Merciful, the Compassionate*).
(*Calligraphic composition*).

AL-GHAZĀLI

The Chapter on the Love of God

In the name of God, the Merciful, the Compassionate! Praise to God who has freed the hearts of His saints from the greed of this world and its false appearance.

Who has purified their secret thoughts from all contemplation except that of His presence;

Then has chosen these hearts for His worship on earth, covered with His Omnipotence;

Then has revealed Himself mystically to them with His Names and His Attributes so that these hearts are inflamed by contact with the rays of His Knowledge;

Then He has unveiled the Majesty of His Face to them so that their hearts are consumed by virtue of the flames of His Love;

Then He has concealed Himself from these hearts by the substance of His Majesty so that they have wandered in the perilous desert of His Sublimity and His Magnificence.

Each time that these hearts have thrilled at the essential spectacle of divine Majesty, the zeal of reason and of its introspection have covered them in helpless amazement.

Each time that these hearts have been tempted to depart, overcome by sadness, a voice from the direction of the Tents of Beauty has called them back, counselling them to have patience.

O thou who despairest of deserving the favour of Truth, this voice said, beware of thy ignorance and precipitation!

For their hearts have remained between refusal and acceptance; between repression and admission, for they have been shipwrecked on the Ocean of His Knowledge and have been consumed by the fire of His Love.

May God extend his benediction over Muḥammad, the seal of the prophets, for the perfection of his prophethood, and over his Companions, the Lords of the creatures, and over his imams, who are the guides of truth and of poor people before Him.

May God grant them all peace!

And then:

Love belongs to God.

It is the most perfect, the most extreme of Stations, the sum of the apogee of Degrees. . . .

Nevertheless certain scholars (*Ulamā*) have denied this possibility, saying: Love has no meaning apart from the value of persevering along the road of submission to God—may He be exalted! As for the very reality of love, it is an improbable thing, except for certain persons and in certain exceptional cases.

In denying love, these scholars have denied Intimacy, the ardent Desire, the sweetness of Confidence and of the attitudes which are involved in loving and all that flows from it.

Of necessity it must throw down all that contains this order of things.

So for this reason we shall record in the present chapter of our work the probative texts of the divine law concerning love, its reality and its causes.

Next, we shall show that none is worthy of love save God—may He be exalted! We shall prove that the supreme enjoyment is to contemplate God—may He be exalted!—face to face. We shall speak of the reasons which show that the joy of contemplating God face to face in the world to come infinitely surpasses the knowledge which we have had of Him here below.

We shall establish the reasons which increase our need of loving God, the various reasons which men have for desiring God, the reasons for the basic incapacity of human intelligence for knowing God—may He be exalted!

We shall go on to expound the exact value of ardent Desire, and to expound the love of God for His servant.

Then we shall come to those verses of the Qur'ān about the signs of the servant's love for God—may He be exalted!

We shall establish the meaning of the Intimacy of God. We shall discuss the rapture which Intimacy brings. We shall record the saying of the Book of God which determines the exact value of Satisfaction.

We shall prove its excellence and then its reality. We shall show that prayer and the horror of sin do not contradict satisfaction. It is the same with the care which is taken to avoid occasions of disobeying (the divine commandments).

Finally will come stories and various incidents concerning Lovers.

The whole Earth is a mass of dry mud, of mud such as the bodies of men. The empires of this world, however great they may be and whatever degree of respect the peoples may have for them, are no more than dust fallen from this dry mud. This dust is itself a favour from God Most High and a thing permitted by Him.

It is absurd then to love one of the servants of God Most High for his power and for the authority which flows from his person, for his ascendancy and for his greatness of soul, and not to love God Most High for the same reasons. There is no might and no power save that of God, the Noble, the Magnanimous!

He is the Sovereign, the Conqueror; the Wise, the Master of the Heavens, holding their ring folded in His right hand.

The Earth, the right to possess something in it, and all that exists in it are shut up in His hand. The locks of hair which fall from the heads of all creatures continue in His powerful grasp. If God were to annihilate these creatures to the lowest one, His Empire would not be lessened by the weight of one little ant. If

He multiplied them a thousand times, this act of creation would not cost Him any trouble.

For no fatigue wearies Him, no effort is hard for Him in His manifestations.

There is no Power save His. He is Powerful through the workings of His own Power.

To Him belong beauty, splendour, grandeur, magnificence, might and mastery!

If man can be tempted to think that he who wields power is loved because of the fulness of his power, let him be careful not to forget that no one can be loved for the fulness of his power save God and God alone.

With regard to the quality which shelters man from vices and imperfections and purifies him from baseness and turpitude, this is one of the conditions of love. It is also one of the exigencies of beauty and of the perfection of the hidden representations of the prophets and of those whose faith is profound. The latter, however, even though they are without blemish and without fault, their sanctity perfect, their purity complete, could not conceive of these virtues except as coming from the One, from Him who is the truth, from the all holy King.

To Him alone belongs majesty! He alone is worthy of worship!

The created being, whatever he may be, is not exempt from faults and imperfections. On the contrary, his condition is to be weak, to have been created from nothing, to be insignificant, and to give way under necessity. He is all vice, all malformation.

Perfection belongs to God, the One. Whoever is not He has no perfection except that which God has measured out to him. He whose perfection has been measured out to him cannot show towards others the generosity of a complete perfection.

Perfection is one of the lowest degrees of the Omnipotence of God.

God is not a servant dependent on someone other than Himself. He is not the helper of anyone. To attribute perfection without any defect to anyone other than God would be nonsensical.

For He has no equal in respect of perfection. He is pure from every malformation. He is preserved from all sin.

It would be too long to enumerate all the ways in which He is holy and in His essential truth is exempt from every blemish.

These notions are one of the mysteries of the sciences which are revealed to the initiated. We shall not delay over them.

Following on this remark, let us say that if there is a beauty and a perfection worthy of being loved, their reality is only fulfilled in God. . . .

In this way then, what is beautiful is to be loved.

Beauty in the absolute sense of the word belongs alone to the One who has no equal, the unique One who has no like, the eternal to whom none is similar, the rich who has no needs, the omnipotent who does what He pleases, and who judges as He will.

No one resists his decrees. No one postpones the execution of His judgements.

Beauty belongs alone to the omniscient, whose knowledge does not omit the weight of one little ant in the heavens or on the earth; the victorious, from underneath whose sovereign hand the necks of the proud will not escape. This sovereign hand will come down upon the Caesars and will seize them by the throat.

Beauty belongs alone to the eternal, whose existence has nothing before it, the eternal, whose duration will have no end, the indispensable by his being, round whose presence the possibility of not being does not flit, He who lives and maintains Himself in life of Himself, by whom every creature is maintained in life, the omnipotent master of the heavens and of the earth, the creator of the minerals, the animals and the vegetables.

Beauty belongs alone to Him who alone has power, who commands the cherubim that bear the throne, the unique, He who alone has the empire, the dispenser of all grace, of all majesty, of all splendour, of all beauty, of all power, of all perfection. He whose majesty dazzles the intelligences when they receive word of it.

Beauty belongs alone to Him whose description makes all tongues dumb. The crown of the knowledge of the initiates is an avowal of the impossibility there is of knowing Him.

The most eminent gift of the prophethood of the prophets is an avowal of inability to describe Him.

God has given this revelation to Moses—peace be upon him!

He undoubtedly lies who claims to have love for Me yet sleeps far from My thought as soon as the night covers him with its shadows.

Every being who loves, does he not aspire to meet with his loved ones?

There am I, quite near, found by him who seeks Me.*

Moses—peace be upon him!—said:

Lord, where art Thou, so that I may come towards Thee?

If thou hast set out with this intention, replied God, thou hast already arrived.†

. . . Whoever loves here below only because he hopes for the lights of Paradise, the houris and the palaces, will be admitted to Paradise. He will go wherever he will. He will play with the young boys and will possess the women, but his enjoyment will be limited to that in the other world.

No man will receive for his share of love except that part which his soul longed for and that which his eye tasted beforehand.

He who looks only to the Master of the House, the Possessor of the Kingdom, and has never been subject except to love for Him in all purity and truth, will be received in the Place of Truth, close to the Omnipotent King.

The righteous will live in abundance in the midst of gardens. They will live a sweet life in Paradise with the houris and the ever-youthful boys.

As for those admitted to intimacy, their attention will be given to the divine presence alone. They will have no eyes except for it. They will despise the delights of Paradise in view of the mediocrity of those who are there, but who for the most part are preoccupied with satisfying their passions and their sensual instincts.

Among those present, there will also be other people.

That is why the Messenger of God—God bless and preserve him!—has said:

The majority of the inhabitants of Paradise are sottish, but in proximity to God in the highest heaven (*'Illiyun*) are the people of understanding.

(I will add, so far as concerns me:)

When intelligence is incapable to grasp the meaning of the word *'Illiyun*, there is something seriously wrong.

God has said (Qur'ān, lxxxiii, 19): Who shall make thee to know what is 'Illiyun?

---

* Cf. 'Be consoled! thou wouldst not seek me unless thou hadst already found me.' (Pascal, *Pensees.*)

† *Ibid.*

'Paradise is a plaything for children'
said Bistami. . . . A single grain of the love of God is
worth more than a hundred thousand paradises.
(Western Turkestan, c. 1500)

Catafalque (Tabut) of the tomb of Sidi 'Abd ar-Rahman at Algiers.

Sanctuary and cemetery of Sidi 'Abd ar-Rahman at Algiers.

SIDI-'ABD AR-RAḤMĀN*

The merits of reciting the Qur'ān

Al-Ghazāli has said, in the chapter on meditation (*Tafakkur*):

For him who is in the way of contemplation which leads to the knowledge, whose fruit is the possession of the glorious states and at the same time preservation from unworthy qualities, there is nothing more efficacious than the attentive recitation of the Qur'ān.

This attentive recitation is meritorious for all qualities and all states.

There is in the Qur'ān a saving medicine for those who are wise.

It is the Qur'ān which inspires fear and hope, resignation and the action of grace, love and ardent desire and the other glorious states.

There is in it that which preserves from qualities that are unworthy.

It is absolutely necessary that the servant should read it, repeating the verse which requires to be repeated as many times as may be necessary, even if he has to spend the whole night doing so.

The reading of a single verse, while putting one's whole heart in it in order to enter thoroughly into its inmost substance and to grasp its full meaning, is worth more than the reading of the Qur'ān from beginning to end without any reflection or any effort to understand it.

Undoubtedly each one of the words of the Qur'ān contains innumerable secrets.

A man does not usefully dwell on a verse unless he has the subtlety of understanding which comes from a pure heart after sincere works.

The attentive study of the traditions of the Messenger of God—God bless and preserve him!—is also of great value.

The generous presence of substantial words has been made there.

Each of these words is one of the oceans of Wisdom.

When he who is wise has meditated on it as it ought to be meditated on, his attention cannot be taken away from it again so long as he lives.

---

* Sidi 'Abd ar-Rahmān al-Tha'alibi, patron of Algiers (1385–1470), *Jawāhir*, from the translation of G. Laurès.

The detailed commentary of the verses and of the traditions will never finish.

Recollect the words of the Messenger of God—God bless and preserve him!

Truly the spirit of wholeness has breathed in my heart.

Cherish whom you will, you will have to leave him. Live how you will, you will have to die.

Do what gives you pleasure, you will receive the just requital for it.

Calligraphic composition repeating four times sura 112 *of the Qur'an:*
Say: It is he, God the one, God the eternal!
He has not begotten and has not been begotten.
He has no equal.

‘UMAR IBN AL-FĀRIḌ

‘Sultan of Lovers’

The greatest Arab mystical poet, Ibn al-Fāriḍ, was born in Cairo, and died there in 1235. His most famous poem is the Khamriyah *in praise of wine, of divine love and of gnosis. His longest and most doctrinal is the* Naẓm as-Suluk *or great* tā’iyah, *dealing with metaphysical realization and the spiritual journey according to the Ṣūfi method. All his* qasīdas *and couplets are in an extremely subtle style, full of puns and clever alliterations which show themselves to be not only suitable for the expression of mystical ideas but indeed favourable to it by the iridescent gleams suggesting relationships between the visible and the invisible. In the same way, ‘the arabesque’ in painting, in decorative sculpture and in music is a wise modulation between Being and Non-being, so to speak, suggesting the fundamental emptiness of the sensible world at the same time as the delights of that world as the manifestation of the one Reality from which it draws all its existence.*

They have been commented on allegorically by numerous interpreters. They contain the fundamental themes of the unity of existence, of the transforming union of Knowledge and Love, and even the renunciation of the graces and of the sensible fervours (stressed by Asin Palacios in the case of the Shādhilite school which seems to have influenced in this respect the Spanish Christian mystics). These themes are caught up into the habitual themes of profane poetry, of ‘udhrite’ or Platonic love, of blame, of censure, of love’s bondage, of dreams, and of devastating and transfiguring love; some of these also occur in the Western troubadours.

The plan of most of the qasīdas (of an average length of about fifty verses) is not rigid. They open with a verse which evokes a nostalgic theme or summarizes the dominant theme or general tonality, like a great Beethoven harmony. But in this tonality, the ideas follow each other without appreciable discursive order, and the verses are often isolated, like the pearls of an undone necklace

Here are some of the verses most characteristic of this great poet, unequalled in a genre much imitated, and characteristic also of Arab mystic poetry in general.

We have drunk to the memory of the Beloved a wine which has intoxicated us before the creation of the vine.

It is limpid and is not of water; it is fluid and is not of air, it is a light without fire and a spirit without body.

Its word has pre-existed eternally in all existing things so that it has neither forms nor images.

It is by means of it that all things here exist. But they veil it with wisdom from him who does not understand.

If you become drunk with this wine, were it but to last an hour, time will be your slave and you will have power.

He has not lived here below who has lived without getting drunk, and he has no sense who has not died of his intoxicating.

My heart tells me that you are my murderer. May my soul be your ransom! whether you know it or not.

I have only my soul (or my life). He who gives his soul for love is not wasteful.

If you accept it, I have reached, thanks to your help, the goal which I should otherwise have lacked.

The passion persists and the union is still awaited; they lose patience and the meeting is delayed.

If union is not possible with thee, promise it at least to my hope and put it off if you have promised and intend not to keep it.

I run towards the breaths of the zephyr to distract myself but my gaze only rises to the face of the one to whom they have borne their perfume.

What does it matter if he seems to remove himself. He whom I love is with me!

Show the proudest coquetry, thou hast the right; conduct thyself as a tyrant; beauty has given thee this power.

If my loss may unite me with thee, ah! make it to come quickly, that I may be thy ransom!

Try my love as much as thou wilt; the choice that I have made is to please thee.

Thou art present in me even in thy absence, and in thy cruelty I feel a tenderness.

How I love that night when I was able to capture thy wandering; my half-sleep was the net that helped me to catch thee.

The full moon has replaced for my awakened eye the image of thy face; in every strange form, thy apparition has refreshed my eyes. I see only thee.

Mystics in a garden. (*Bodleian Library, Oxford. Ms. Elliot* 339, *f.* 95 *verso*)

Take the remains of what thou hast left of thyself; there is no goodness in love if it leaves a drop of blood in the heart.

Welcome to him of whose visit I am not worthy! The word of the messenger is: after despair, deliverance.

There is good news for thee! Raise up what is on thee! Despite thy imperfection, thou hast been summoned above.

It is He, Love! Spare thy heart. Passion is not an easy thing, without danger. If someone chooses it, is he quite sane?

Live freely; love's rest is a fatigue, its beginning an illness and its end, death.

For me, however, death by love is life; I give thanks to my Beloved for having offered it to me.

If you wish to live happily, die a martyr. If not, Love will know not to find other victims.

If She unfolds my body, She will see in it all substance, in that all heart, in that all love.

With Her, a year is but a trice, but the moment when she turns away is for me a year.

Is it the glow of lightning which shines in the plain? Is it a torch which has been lit on the heights of Nejd?

Or is it Lailah the 'Āmirīyah, who, drawing back her veil, has changed dusk into dawn?

Love is the whole of life. Thou wilt perish because of it. It is thy lot to die of it, and thy excuse.

JAMI

The hidden Treasure and the dialectic of love

Jami (Jāmi), the great Persian poet, who died at Herat in 1492, in his Yūsuf and Zulaika *(Fr. tr. by Bricteux, Paris, 1927) groups around the loves of Joseph and of the wife of Potiphar, all sorts of anecdotes, effusions and mystical definitions. Starting from the 'sacred' ḥadīth, 'I was a hidden Treasure' . . . he expresses the Ṣūfi dialectic of the manifestation, and re-discovers the Platonic dialectic of love.*

Absolute Beauty, free from the shackles of appearances, is only revealed of itself and by its own light.`. . . No mirror has ever reflected its features; no comb has ever dressed its hair. Its eye is not acquainted with the dust of kohl. No nightingale had neighboured with its rose and no fly enhanced its freshness. No eye had contemplated it, even in imagination. She sang to herself of her beauty, and played with herself a game of love.

But Beauty cannot bear to remain ignored behind the curtain; a beautiful face has a horror of the veil and, if you shut the door on it, will go and appear at the window. See how the tulip on the mountain-top, at the first sign of spring, pierces the rocks with its stem, showing us its beauty. And you yourself, when a rare idea appears in your mind, you are obsessed by it and must express it in word or writing. Such is the natural impulse of Beauty wherever it may exist. Eternal Beauty had to submit itself and emerged from the sacred regions of mystery to light up the horizons and the souls. A light from her shot out over the earth and the skies. She revealed herself in the mirror of beings. All the atoms making up the universe became like so many mirrors, each one reflecting an aspect of the eternal splendour. A parcel of its light fell on the rose, which made the nightingale sick with love. It communicated its ardour to a torch where a thousand moths had just burnt themselves. It was to her that Lailah was indebted for her charms, Lailah whose every hair bound the heart of Majnūn. It is she who gave to the lips of Shirin the sweetness which ravished Parviz and Farhad and to the moon of Canaan (Joseph) the sweet light which infatuated Zulaikah. Such is the beauty that is visible through the veil of terrestrial beauties and ravishes all the hearts smitten by

The poet Jami seated with his friends.
(Miniature attributed to Behzad. Collection Bernard Berenson)

love. It is love for her that revives the hearts and fortifies the souls. At bottom it is by her that every amorous heart is really smitten, whether this is admitted or not. . . .

Just as beauty does, so love emanates from her if it shows itself in you. If you consider her closely, she is the mirror, she is at the same time the treasure and the casket. The 'You' and the 'I' are displaced here and are only vain appearances. Be silent, for this is a boundless subject that not even a genius can treat worthily. Let us confine ourselves to loving and suffering in silence, for without this we are but worthless. The heart which is exempt from the sickness of love is not a heart; the body deprived of the grief of love is only water and lemon. It is amorous disquietude, which gives to the universe its eternal movement; it is the dizziness of love which makes the spheres turn round.

If you want to be free, be love's captive. If you want joy, open your chest to the suffering of love. The wine of love gives heat and drunkenness; without it, there is frozen selfishness. You may follow many ideals but only love will deliver you from yourself. . . . It is the only way which leads to truth.

I have heard it said that a disciple went to find a shaikh to ask him to guide him in the spiritual way, and the old man said to him: 'If your foot has never trodden the path of love, go and know love, then come back and find me. Sniff at first the cup of the wine of appearances, if you want afterwards to savour the draught of the mystical liquor; but do not delay too long at appearances; cross this bridge quickly if you want to arrive at the supreme goal.'

FARĪD AD-DĪN 'AṬṬĀR

The language of the birds

The metaphysic of Unity was elaborated by the Ṣūfis on the basis of some Qur'ānic verses in the atmosphere of the conquered empires and under the influence of knowledge acquired for ascetic traditions which invited rivalry, and of philosophical notions and terms inherited from Greek. Despite the peculiar turn given to this metaphysic by the Ṣūfis, which is very marked, it is close to the traditions of universal spiritual experience. Here is what became of this metaphysic of Unity under the pen of the great Persian poets of the thirteenth century, six hundred years after the Hijrah.

The poem of Farīd ad-Dīn 'Aṭṭār (Mantiq at-Ṭā'ir, *Language of the Birds) who died at Nishāpūr at the time of the Mongol Conquest, suggests, with its numerous picturesque anecdotes, dramatic, lyrical, or elegiac, its dialogues and its theoretical reflections, the mysterious flights of birds led by the Hoopoe in the quest for the Simurgh of the Absolute Essence across the various mystical valleys towards those of annihilation and unification. It was translated into French in 1857 by Garcin de Tassy.*

As he placed the earth on the back of a bull, the bull is on the fish and the fish is in the air. But what does the air rest on? On nothing; but nothing is nothing and all that is nothing. Admire the work of this king although he never considered himself as anything but a pure nonentity. In fact, since His essence exists uniquely (by Itself, in Reality) there is certainly nothing outside it. His throne is on the water and the world is in the air; but leave the water and the air, for all is of God. The Throne and the world are only a talisman. God is all that and these things have only a nominal value (God is the real Being and the reality of Existence, beings taking their being from Him. Know that He is the visible and invisible world. There is no (absolute Being) but He, and what is, is He. But alas! it is not possible for anyone to see Him. Our eyes are blind although the world is lit by a brilliant sun. If you succeed in glimpsing Him, you lose your wisdom; if you see Him entirely, you lose yourself. . . . O Thou Whom one sees not although Thou makest Thyself known, all the world art Thou and

The mystical poet and hagiographer Farid-ad-Din 'Attar
(Sixteenth Century, Bodleian Library Oxford. Ms. Ouseley add 24, f. 78 verso)

نمودند جوان نیز روانماند خود را بدیشان رساند بخدمت حضرت خواجه عبد الله انصاری

رسیدند و خرقه از دست او پوشیدند مجلس بیست و دوم سحاب افاضت آثار گوهر

بار و در دریای مواج اسرار شیخ فرید الدین عطار دریایی بوده پر از جواهر حقایق و اسرار در اول

حال بطلب اشتغال می نموده اند و دونانی بسیار در گرد آنحضرت بوده دکان عطاری داشته اند

پر از اشربه و ادویه و متاع آن کار خود در دکان می نشسته اند روزی درویشی بر دکان آن

nothing other than Thee is manifest. (The world is the manifestation of the divine attributes.) The soul is hidden in the body and thou art hidden in the soul. O Thou Who art hidden in what is hidden, O soul of the soul, Who art more than all and before all. Everything sees by Thee and Thou art seen in all things. Although Thou art treasure hidden in the soul, nevertheless Thou art manifest in soul and body. O Thou Who art in the exterior and in the interior of the soul, Thou art not and Thou art all I have said. . . .

Science and ignorance are here the same thing, for this being cannot be explained or described. Thou shouldst be able to recognize God by Himself, not by thyself; it is He who opens the way which leads to Him, not human wisdom. Annihilate thyself, such is perfection. Renounce thyself, that is the measure of thy union with Him, and that is all. . . .

Many people know the surface of this ocean, but they ignore its depth. Now there is a treasure in this depth and the visible world is the talisman which protects it, but this talisman of bodily shackles will at last be broken. Thou will find the Treasure when the Talisman has disappeared; the soul will manifest itself when the body shall have been laid aside. But thy spirit is another talisman; it is for this mystery another substance. Walk in the way which I show thee and do not ask for an explanation; do not ask a remedy for such an ill. . . . O God, who is infinite if it is not Thou? Who is like Thee without limit and without bounds? I am in the tumultuous ocean of the world. Ah! rescue Thy servant from this sea which is foreign to him! Thou didst throw me into it Thyself; now rescue me. Concupiscence seized my whole being completely. If Thou dost not reach out Thy hand to me, alas, what will become of me? Good comes of Thee but evil of me. Believers and unbelievers are equally immersed in blood; their head turns and they are mad. Ah! be a guide! One who has had the good fortune to enter the way has become disgusted with himself and has lost himself in Thee. O Thou Whose tenderness is like that of a mother! O Thou Who art full of tenderness towards the children of Thy Way, throw a kind glance on those who are submerged. Have pity on our heart full of agony; come to our aid when Thou seest the waters engulf us!

(*The desires and the courage of the birds engaged in the quest are unequal. The nightingale would content himself with the love of the perishable rose; the parrot only searches for the water of immortality, the peacock only desires the joys of Paradise. The Hoopoe always proclaims that the real end is beyond.*)

Admire thy King with thy own heart. See His throne is an atom. All appearance is the mysterious shadow of Simurgh. Simurgh is not distinct from his shadow. Both exist together. Therefore seek them reunited, or rather, leave the shadow and then you will find the secret. If good fortune aids you, you will see in this shadow the sun; but if you were to lose yourself in this shadow, how would you be able to obtain the Simurgh himself?

The Simurgh and the Dragon. (*Western Turkestan, about* 1400)

O cup-bearer, fill my cup with the blood of my heart, and if there is no more, give me the dregs that remain. Love is a cruel grief which devours all. The more it tears the veil of the soul, the more it mends it again. An atom of love is preferable to all which exists between the horizons. Love is the marrow of our beings but it does not exist without sorrow. . . .

Whoever is born, dies. You have been nourished to die; you you have been brought into this world to be taken away. The sky is like a bowl upside down which is immersed each evening in the blood of the evening sky. It seems that the sun, armed with a sword, is ordered to cut off the heads of all who are under this

Majnun the Fool of Lailah follows the processional circles (tawaf) round the Ka'bah. (Ms. Persian, B.N.)

bowl. Pure or impure, you are only a drop of water kneaded with earth. How should you want to dispute with the ocean this drop of water which is only sadness? Even if throughout your life you had been a ruler in this world, you would have to give over your soul to affliction and groaning. . . .

(*Majnūn was the Fool of Lailah, who wandered in the desert, driven mad by the love of his cousin, and became the model of 'Udhrite love, the Platonic love of the Banū 'Udhra, who died when they loved.*)

'Majnūn was seen one day, sifting the sand with his hands. 'What do you seek thus?' someone asked him. 'I seek Lailah'. 'Are you hopeful of finding Lailah thus?' 'Would such a pure pearl

Qais becomes mad (*Majnun*) *and dies of love for his cousin Lailah.* '*He who remains chaste and dies of love, dies a martyr,*' *says a hadith attributed to the Prophet.* (*Iran,* 16*th century*)

be found in this dust?' 'I seek Lailah everywhere,' replied Majnūn, 'in the hope of finding her somewhere some day.'*

(*The birds in the valley of unification:*)

Do you see double? Would you see several objects if you were not squint-eyed? The eye of man does not see there anything accessible to the senses. There is neither Ka'bah nor pagoda. Learn the true doctrine; the eternal existence of the infinite Being. We see no other save Him, recognize as permanent no other. We are in Him and by Him and with Him. . . .

In so much as you will live to yourself, good and evil will exist for you. But when you lose yourself (in the sun and the divine essence) all will be love. . . . The serpent and the scorpion are in you, behind the veil, asleep, but if you touch them, ever so little, each of them will have the force of a hundred dragons. Thus there is for each of us a Hell full of serpents. If you do not act, they act infernally. If you secure yourself against these vile animals, you will sleep peaceably on the earth; if not, these serpents and these scorpions will murder you violently even under the dust of the tomb at the Last Day.

When the traveller has entered this valley, he disappears, just like the earth he tramples on. He will be lost because the unique being will be manifest; he will remain dumb because this Being will speak. The part will become the whole; or rather there will be neither part nor whole. He who has learnt something of this secret turns his head from the kingdom of the two worlds; but such an individual is not found in the world, and shall one there find the fragrance of this secret? The being whom I proclaim does not exist in isolation; all the world is this Being; existence or non-existence, it is always this Being.

(*Only thirty birds arrive there and, like the Phoenix, find in annihilation the beginning of a new existence. The shadow is lost in the sun; there is no longer either guide or traveller; even the road has ceased to exist.*)

---

* *Two famous verses:*

Say not her dwelling is to the East of Nejd; all Nejd is a dwelling for the 'Āmiriyah (*Lailah, of the tribe of Banu 'Āmir*).

She has a place near every water-hole; a trace of her remains near every abandoned camp.

When the ocean of immensity agitates its waves, how shall the figures traced on its surface exist? These figures are none other than the present world and the world to come. He whose heart is lost in this ocean is lost there for always and will remain there at rest. In this calm sea he will find nothing but the fanā'.* If he is ever permitted to return from his annihilation, he will know the meaning of creation, and many secrets will be revealed to him.

The wood of aloes and the wood of heating put in the fire are both reduced to cinders. Under two forms, they are in fact the same thing, and nevertheless their qualities are very distinct. A filthy object is not helped by falling into an ocean of rosewater; it will remain in its degradation because of its own character. But if a pure thing falls into this ocean, it will lose its special existence, and will participate in the movement of the waves of this ocean; in ceasing to exist alone, it will henceforth be beautiful. It exists and does not exist. How can that happen? It is impossible for the spirit to conceive it.

IBN 'ARABI

The great esoteric writer of the thirteenth century, Muḥyi 'd-Dīn ibn 'Arabi, in his Meccan Revelations (Futuḥāt al-Makkiyāt) (*Bulaq, 1270/1854, ii, 408*) *examines the metaphysical senses of the* samā' (*hearing, music*), *whence comes the mystical and initiatory role of poetry and of the spiritual concert.*

The origin of our existence is our hearing of His *fiat* (*kun*). The first thing that we have heard from the Truth is His Word, and existence has resulted from it. Thus it is in the (mystic) Way; when there is a samā', if there is no ecstasy at this hearing, and if this ecstasy does not realize existential unity, it is not a true samā' of the category to which the people of God refer. When God says to a thing which is still non-existent: '*Kun!* Be!' this is what the people of the samā' realize. The word which they hear and which produces the unifying ecstasy and fills their heart with the divine knowledge, corresponds to the *fiat* which has produced their existence (*wujūd*, existence; *wajd*, ecstasy). For them ecstasy precedes existence. The 'general' transcendental samā' may be

* Valley of the *fanā'*, extinction, annihilation, 'nirvana'.

Dancers seized by the 'wonder' ('ajab) collapsing on the ground and being held by the waist (Bodleian Library, Oxford)

divine, spiritual or natural. The first is that of the secret ones. For them all that exists comes from divine Words, and the divine Words cannot pass away.

Corresponding to these are the auditions which can no more cease. These auditions take place in their 'secret' (*sirr*, fine point of the soul) by the very existence of these words. God has said: 'Each time that they receive a word from their Lord, they listen.' This 'station' of the samā', which all do not reach, but which some pass, corresponds to the Names of God which are numberless. For each Name there is a tongue, and for each tongue a word. And the essence is one of the Speaker and the listener. When there is a call we yield ourselves to it; thus He has said: 'Ask me and I shall hearken to you.' He hears us, and after the prostration of the prayer we say: 'God hears him who praises Him.' Some speak by God and others by themselves, but at bottom it is the same thing for in Existence there is only God. There is no Speaker and listener but God (may He be exalted!). . . . .

The spiritual samā' consists of the action of the divine pens on the book of existence. Existence is an unfolded leaf and the world is a book; the pen speaks, the intelligences hear, the words inscribe themselves and become testimony, and the essence of the testimony is the essence of understanding.

Muhammad Tabadkami in ecstasy dancing to tambourines and flute. (*Bodleian Library, Oxford. Ms. Ouseley add.* 24, *f.* 119 *recto*)

The natural samā‘ is based on four realities. Nature is fourfold, with subjects and objects, and active and passive; there are four directions and four humours, to which correspond four basic musical sounds, which make them (the humours) move and produce musical pleasure. The pleasure of these sounds and their effect on characters have their root in the divine Word. He who hears a sound suited to his temperament cannot escape from its influence.

Are the fuqahā' (*plural of* faqih, *lawyer*) *going to forbid us to listen to the song of the birds? asks 'Abd al-Ghani an-Nābulsi* (Idāh ad-Ḍilālāt, *Damascus, 1302/1885*), *who in the eighteenth century wrote a commentary on the great mystical poet Ibn al-Fāriḍ.*

Music is not unlawful unless it is a vain distraction involving the neglect of a duty. It is not right to condemn it in itself, nor to judge arbitrarily those who love it. (*Heidegger speaks also of a music which 'distracts' and a music which 'leads to finding'.*) *Besides there are lawful distractions which may produce a sincere and pure act of grace. The pleasure of music even distracts from vulgar pleasures those who are not capable of contenting themselves with pure divine joy. If it is unlawful when it troubles souls and incites them to debauchery, but permitted and indifferent in other cases, it is commendable for the sincere ṣūfi since it stimulates his love for God.*

مدام و بچد و سر جان ز عشق او شده ام
یکی غریب و دوم عاشق و سیوم رسوا
غریب و عاشق و رسوا چنان شدم که شدند
یکی چو بشر و دوم وامق و سیوم عذرا
چو بشر و وامق و عذرا ز من بیاموزند
یکی فغان و دویم ناله و سیوم سودا

JALĀL AD-DĪN AR-RŪMI

and the Dance of Ecstasy

Jalāl ad-Dīn ar-Rūmi, the celebrated founder of the Mevlevis (Mawlāwis) or whirling dervishes, whose tomb Maurice Barrès went to visit at Konia (Anatolia), was born at Balkh in 1207 and died at Konia in 1273 in the time of the Seljūks, after a long life dedicated to poetry, to music and to the dance of ecstasy. Under the influence of a very mysterious initiator, Shams ad-Din of Tabriz, he adopted the circular astral dance, a sort of waltz in six-time, with an orchestra consisting notably of the German flute, the lute and the violin; earlier he had danced with contortions of the body and movements of the arms, doubtless a little in the manner of the Rifā'is. His disciples have developed a musical culture of a very high order, and their repertoire has been taken down in part by the Turkish musicologist Ra'ūf Yekta Bey. His biographers assure us that he himself was capable of whirling for hours and days. The story is preserved of a gold-beater, at the rhythm of whose beating the saint had entered into dancing ecstasy, and who continued to beat until he had destroyed his gold leaf, since he did not want to interrupt the 'state' of Jalāl ad-Dīn.

Dervish dance at Constantinople.

Jalal ad-Dīn ar-Rumi and the gold-beater. (16*th century. Bodleian Library, ms. Ouseley add.* 24, *f.* 78).

Though no doubt of Turkish origin, he composed a number of poems in Persian, notably the Divān-i-Shams-i-Tabriz *and the famous* Mathnawi *containing twenty-six thousand couplets, rhyming two by two.**

Our musics are the echo of the hymns which the spheres sing as they revolve. . . . The song of the worlds which evolve, this is what men try to reproduce with the lute and with the voice. We have all heard the lofty melodies in the paradise which we have lost, and although the earth and the water have overwhelmed us, we retain our memory of the songs of the sky. He who loves feeds his love by listening to music, for music reminds him of the joys of his first union with God. . . .

Listen to the reed flute, to what it has to say and its laments on the subject of separation. Since they cut me, it says, in the reeds of the marsh, men and women complain at my voice. My heart is torn by desertion; it is in order that I may be able to express the grief caused by desire. Everyone who remains far from his original source looks for the time when reunion will operate anew. . . . The complaint of the lute is of the fire and not only of the air. He who is deprived of this fire is as one dead. It is the fire of love which inspires the flute. . . . The flute is the confidante of unhappy lovers. It has bared my most intimate secrets. Who has seen a poison and an antidote like that of the flute? . . .

Rise up, O son! break your bonds and be free. How much longer will you remain the prisoner of silver and gold? . . . Salutations to thee, Love, O sweet folly! You who heal all our infirmities, who are the surgeon of our pride and presumption, our Plato and our Galen. Love raises our earthly bodies towards the sky and makes even the hills dance with joy. . . . If my Beloved only touch me with his lips, I too, like the flute, shall burst into melody. . . . My Beloved is all in all, the lover only the veil. The Beloved is all that lives, the lover a dead thing. . . . Love desires that its secret be revealed, for if a mirror reflects nothing, what use is it? It is because the rust has not been cleaned off. If it had been cleaned of all rust and all dirt, it would reflect the rays of the light of God. . . .

Love is the astrolabe of the divine mysteries. A lover may desire

---

* The *Mathnawi* has been translated into English by E. H. Whinfield (abridged), London, 1887, 1898, and Sir James Redhouse, 1881 (continued by Wilson, 1910); cf. E. G. Browne, *A Literary History of Persia*, ii, 515ff.

this or that love, but in the end he is drawn towards the King of Love.

Happy the soul who for the love of God has left family and riches, has destroyed his house to find the hidden Treasure, and with this treasure has reconstructed it, more beautiful than before. . . . Yes, the business of religion is nothing other than losing one's way, not that which comes from turning away from God, but that which immerses you and absorbs you in Him.

It is the divine word which has given being to things, which makes them unfold from nothingness and makes return to it. It speaks to the ear of the rose and it opens out. It speaks to the tulip and it flowers.

A man knocked at the door of the Friend. 'Who is there?' 'It is I.' 'There is no room here for two,' answered the Voice. The man went away and spent a year in solitude. When he returned, 'Who is there,' said the Voice. 'It is you, O Beloved.' 'Since it is I, then I enter! There is no room for two "I's" in a house!'

Since non-being is the mirror of being, if you are wise, choose self-denial. . . . Non-being and the imperfect are the mirrors of Beauty in all things. Non-being is a clear filtered essence in which all beings are infused. The defects are the mirrors of the attributes of Beauty. The imperfect is the mirror of the High and Glorious One. For opposites reveal their opposites, just as the sweetness of honey is shown by the acidity of vinegar. He who recognizes and confesses his faults advances rapidly on the road to perfection. But let not him who imagines himself to be perfect advance towards the Almighty. No worse ill than to imagine that you are perfect can infest your soul. Let fall tears of blood from your eyes and from your heart so that this may drive all self-satisfaction away from you. The fault of Iblis consists in saying: 'I am better than he [Adam].' And the same weakness is hidden in the soul of all creatures.

(*Love which strives for permanence and allows constancy cannot be satisfied with perishable forms.*)

O lover of the light of the sun, do not give your heart to the stones of the wall which reflect it. Distinguish the true dawn from the false one. Distinguish the colour of the wine from that of the cup. . . . The true workman is hidden in his workshop. Go into this workshop and see him face to face. In so far as a veil is drawn over this workman by his work, you cannot see him outside his work. Since his workshop is the dwelling of the Only Wise, whoever searches for it independently, ignores Him. Then come into His workshop which is perishing, in order to be able to see the Creator and Creation at the same time. . . . The slave of the senses who indulges his body imagines that every other man is his enemy, whereas it is his own body that is his enemy. He who triumphs over this enemy is at peace with all men.

(*Sincere love is the most perfect praise and the discursive conception of God that the scholars make for themselves are hardly less adequate than the most homely. An ignorant shepherd said to God: 'Where art Thou, that I may serve Thee? That I may mend Thy boots, that I may comb Thy hair? I shall bring Thee my best milk.' 'Infidel!' said Moses to him, who happened to pass by. 'You are saying foolish, wicked things. God has no need of that. It is insulting to Him to attribute to Him these needs.' The confused shepherd fled to the desert and God reprimanded His prophet:*)

'You have just taken from me one of My servants. You were sent to unite, not to separate. . . . We have given to each one his own character, his peculiar language. What is praise for him is reproof for you. . . . As for Me, I am above all purity or impurity. It is not to gain profit that I have created beings but to show My benevolence towards them. . . . I am not purified by their praises; these are they who have become more pure. I do not consider the exterior and the words, but the state of the heart and the interior. . . . For the heart is the substance and the words are the accidents. The accidents are only the means, the substance is the final cause. A burning heart is what I demand. Therefore do not treat as a sinner a lover who expresses himself badly. One does not wash the bloody body of the martyrs. Blood is worth more than water for a martyr. . . . There is no need to turn towards the Ka'ba when one is inside.

When the love of God rises in your heart, do not doubt that God also feels love for you. You cannot clap your hands with a single hand. The thirsty man cries: 'Where is the delicious water?' God has predestined that we should love eternally. The sky is the man and the earth is the woman.

Yes, all the fish of the sea, the birds of the air, the elephants, the wolves and the lions of the forests, the dragons, the serpents and even the little mice, yes, the air, the earth and the fire take their substance from Him. At each moment the sky cries to Him: 'O Lord, do not for a single instant cease to hold me. Thy help is the pillar of my being.' . . .

Ah! seek help from Him and from no other than Him. Look for water in the ocean, not in a dried-up canal.

The qubbah in the desert.
Memorial of Bayazid Bistami,
the great Iranian mystic of the 9th century.

Turkish calligraphic composition of the 19th century. The text is double as if reflected in a mirror.

MAXIMS, ANECDOTES AND VERSES

All the worlds are but a faint perfume from the Rose of eternity (Nābulsi, in Jabarti, *Merveilles biographiques*, Cairo, 1889, ii, 32).

He who would contemplate the glory of God, let him contemplate a red rose (Wāsiṭi).

What a difference between going to the marriage for the banquet and going to the marriage to be with the Beloved! (Yaḥyā Mu'ādh ar-Rāzi).

God is beautiful and loves beauty.

The world is a tasty fruit. God has lent it to you to see what you will do with it.

The world is prison for the believer and paradise for the unbeliever.

The house where Thou dwellest has no need of other lamp.
Thy longed-for Face shall be our proof on the day when men undertake proofs.
Tomorrow when man and woman will enter into the assembly of judgement, faces will be yellow with fear of the reckoning to be made. I will present myself before Thee, holding my love in my hand, and I shall say: my reckoning should be made according to my love (Rūmi, quoted by Goldziher, *Vorlesungen*).

A moment of love is worth more than seventy years of worship without love (Yaḥyā ar-Rāzi).

God pardons a hundred times. But He keeps His supreme mercy for him whose piety has spared the smallest of creatures (Muḥammad ibn Yūsuf as-Sanūsi of Tlemcen, fifteenth century).

Those who love one another in Me will, on the Day of Judgement, be under the shadow of My throne, on the day when there will be no shadow save Mine ('sacred' ḥadīth, quoted by Ghazāli and Safūri).

The spirits are armed forces. Those who have known one another (above) come together (below); those which repulsed one another, oppose one another (ḥadīth of Platonic character).

He who seeks Me finds Me. He who finds Me knows Me. He who knows Me loves Me. Him who loves Me, I love. Him whom I love I kill. Him whom I kill, it is I who ransom. Him whom I have to ransom, it is I who am his ransom ('sacred' ḥadīth attributed to Sayyidna 'Ali).

All that brings My worshipper closer to Me is more pleasing to Me than the fulfilment of the duties I have prescribed for him.

My worshipper will never cease to come near to Me by supererogatory prayers so that I will love him; and when I love him, I will be his ear with which he hears, his eye with which he sees, his hand with which he strikes, and his foot with which he walks (ḥadīth transmitted by Abu Hurairah, Bukhāri, iv, 296).

Justice without religion is worth more for the order of the universe than the tyranny of a pious prince (Jāmi, *Beharistan* and *Salaman and Absal*, Fr. tr. by Bricteux).

I think that the lily is a child of the fairies, noble and gifted with a lofty eloquence. It certainly possesses a tongue, but it is not allowed to speak to us of the eternal mystery (Salmān de Sâvé, fourteenth century, in Azad, *L'Aube de l'Esperance*).

O Love, destroy not the Ka'bah, for there the travellers, wearied with the journey, rest a moment (Faizi, in *Ain-i-Akbari* by Abu-'l-Fadl 'Allāmi, tr. Blochmann, Calcutta, 1873, i, 554).

The 'external' of the Law is impiety disguised, and the 'real' of impiety is divine wisdom (Hallāj, *Akhbār al-Hallāj*, ed. Massignon, No. 41).

A man once in the presence of Solomon met Azrael, the Angel of Death, who looked at him with fury, so it seemed to him. The man, terrified, asked Solomon to have him transported to the furthest Indies by the winds which obeyed him. Solomon granted his request, and then asked the Angel about him. 'It was not fury that I showed,' he said, 'but astonishment, since God has bidden me take his soul this very day in the Indies, and I was surprised to find him here so far away. I must go immediately to the Indies to kill him.' (Rūmi, *Mathnavi*, 1)

Junaid was asked what the *'ārif* (the initiated, knower, gnostic) is. He said: 'The colour of water is that of its receptacle'.

'Half of Knowledge,' said Abu 'Uthmān al-Makki, 'is the question; the other half is the answer.'

Abu Bakr ash-Shibli said: 'The beginning of this "affair" is Knowledge, *Ma'rifah*, and its end is Unification, *Tawḥīd*.' 'And

The justice of the King.
(The Treasury of Secrets, by Nizami; 17th century Persian ms., B.N.)

what are the marks of Knowledge?' 'Love, *Maḥabbah*, is one, for he who knows Him loves Him.'

God is the reality of existing things (Ibn Sab'in of Murcia, thirteenth century).

None says 'I' except God; for real personality belongs to God alone (Abu Naṣr Sarrāj, *Luma'*).

It has been said: Love commands that you efface your track so well when you leave it, that nothing is left to bring you back from yourself to yourself (Ghazāli, *Iḥyā'*, iv, tr. Laurès).

A fool of God, illuminated (*majdūb*), repulses al-Khidr (a prophet, Elijah), who has drunk at the Source of Life and become immortal. 'For me,' he cries, 'I sacrifice all the days of my life, for I cannot live far from the Beloved' ('Aṭṭār, *Language of Birds*, 64).

The water of immortality is in sight, and the pail is on our lips. The mirror is opposite and Our image is not reflected there (Feghāni, tr. Azad).

You ask where Lailah is, and Lailah glows within you (Ḥarraq, North African mystical poet).

Thy place in my heart is my whole heart; naught save Thee has any place there. My spirit holds Thee between my skin and my bones, see, if I were to lose Thee, how would I fare?
Thy Spirit is mingled with my spirit, as wine is united with pure water.
So, when a thing touches Thee, it touches me!
Thus, then, Thou, it is I, in everything!
I have become Him whom I love and He whom I love has become me! We are two spirits infused into one body.
So to see me is to see Him, and to see Him is to see us.
Between Thee and me there is an 'it is I' which torments me. Oh! By Thy 'it is I' take away my 'it is I' from between us!
Thy image is in my eye, Thy mention on my lips, Thy dwelling in my heart, but where then hast Thou hidden Thyself? (Ḥallāj, *Diwān*, ed. Massignon, 1931).

Ibn 'Aṭā' said: 'We knew God by His works and His attributes; but without a reference we could not know His Reality.' God has said in the Qur'ān: 'Their knowledge cannot comprehend Him.' And this saying of the caliph Abu Bakr is reported: Praise be to God who has given His creatures no way of knowing Him except their incapacity for knowing Him!' (*via negationis*) (Sarrāj, *Luma*', 232, 35).

'He who knows God most,' said Dhu 'n-Nūn al-Miṣri, 'is he who is most puzzled about Him.' 'I have known my Lord by my Lord, and without my Lord I could not have known my Lord.' 'Acknowledge substance of Him,' he said also, 'but deny place of Him; everything that comes into your mind, God is different from that' (Sarrāj, Safūri, Qushairi).

A *faqīr* asked a shaikh to teach him the Supreme Name of God which gives omnipotence. 'Are you worthy of it?' asked the shaikh. 'Yes, indeed.' 'Well, go to the gate of the town, sit down, watch what happens and come and tell me.' The faqir went to the place indicated and sat for some time. An old wood-cutter came along driving an ass laden with wood. A soldier stopped him, took the wood from him, beat him, and drove him and his ass away.

The disciple came back to his master and told him what had happened. The shaikh said to him: 'If you had known the Supreme Name, what would you have done to the soldier?' 'I would have asked for his death,' he replied at once. 'Well,' said the shaikh, 'know that this old wood-cutter is precisely the master who once taught me the Supreme Name.'

In fact the Supreme Name is only useful for those who have patience, self-control, goodwill towards all creatures, and all the virtues found in the saints of God (may He be pleased with them and grant that we profit from their merits!) (Yāfi'i, *Rawd*, 238).

'Praise be to God the Lord of the Worlds, the Merciful, the Compassionate!'

Chosroes Parviz, King of Persia, contemporary with Muhammad (Sassanid cup of silver gilt) Collection of Luynes, B.N.)

SOME DATES

531–579	Chosroes Anushirwan, Sassanid King of Persia.
571	Year of the Elephant. Probable birth of Muḥammad.
590–628	Chosroes Parviz.
610–641	Heraclius, Byzantine Emperor.
*c.*612	Beginning of the Prophet's mission.
614	The Persians at Jerusalem. They carry off the true cross.
622	Hijrah. Muḥammad at Medina.
624	Battle of Badr.
624	Change of Qiblah; the Muslims pray in the direction of Mecca instead of that of Jerusalem.
625	Victories of Heraclius over the Persians.
628	Peace between Heraclius and Siroes; restoration of the true cross.
630	Capture of Mecca.
631	Pilgrimage of Farewell.
632	Death of Muḥammad.
632–634	Caliphate of Abū Bakr.
634–644	Caliphate of 'Umar.
638	Capture of Jerusalem.
642	Victory of Nehavend over the Persians and capture of Alexandria
644–656	Caliphate of 'Uthmān.
656–661	Caliphate of 'Alī.
657	Battle of Ṣiffīn. Beginnings of the Khārijite schism.
661–750	Dynasty of the Umayyads in Damascus.
665	Arab attack on the Maghrib.
670	Foundation of Kairouan by 'Uqbah.
680	Massacre of Kerbelā.
691	Dome of the Rock or Mosque of 'Umar at Jerusalem.
707	The Arabs on the Indus.
708	Conquest of the Balearic Islands.
711	Ṭāriq crosses the Straits of Gibraltar.
718	The Arabs repulsed before Constantinople.
728	Death of Ḥasan al-Baṣri, forerunner of Sūfism.
732	Battle of Poitiers.
756–1031	Dynasty of the Umayyads in Spain.
750–1258	Dynasty of the 'Abbāsids in Baghdad.

754	Iconoclastic Council of Constantinople.
767	Death of Abū Ḥanīfah, founder of the Hanafite rite.
777	Death of the ascetic Ibrahīm Ibn Adham.
786–809	Hārūn ar-Rashīd.
785	Mosque of Cordova.

Mosque of Cordova.

787	Second Council of Nicaea condemning the iconoclasts.
786–922	Idrisids in Morocco.
795	Death of Mālik, founder of the Malikite rite.
800	Charlemagne Emperor of the West.
800–909	Dynasty of the Aghlabites in Ifrīqiyah.
813–833	The caliph Ma'mūn fosters sciences and translations in Baghdad.
820	Death of Shāfi'i, founder of the Shāfi'ite rite.
827	Ptolemy translated into Arabic.
830	Foundation of the 'House of Wisdom' at Baghdad.

838	Capture of Amorium from the Byzantines.
846	Saracens before Rome.
855	Death of Ibn Ḥanbal, founder of the Ḥanbalite rite.
870	Death of the traditionist Al-Bukhārī.
c.**873**	Death of the philosopher Al-Kindi.
873	Death of the traditionist Muslim.
886	Death of Scotus Erigena, translator in the West of the Pseudo-Dionysius Areopagite.
890–931	Movement of the Qarmatians.
c.**909**	Fall of the Rustumid kingdom, 'Ibādite, Khārijite.
909	Fāṭimids in North Africa at Tahert-Tiaret.
922	Execution of the mystic Al-Ḥallāj.
923	Death of the great doctor Rhazes.
935	Death of the theologian Al-Ash'arī.
950	Death of the philosopher, scholar and musician, Al-Fārābī.
969	Faṭimids in Egypt.
980–1037	Avicenna (Ibn Sīna).
994–1064	Ibn Ḥazm of Cordova.
c. **1027**	He composes the *Dove's Neckband*, an essay on love and love poetry.
1039	Seljuk Turks. Tughril Bey, lieutenant of the Caliph of Baghdad.
1055–1147	Almoravids.
1062	Yūsuf ibn Tashfīn founds Marrākesh.
1092	The Cid at Valencia.
1099	First Crusade, Capture of Jerusalem.

Headpiece of pulpit (minbar) of the Great Mosque of Nedroma, donated by a son of the Almoravid, Yusuf ibn Tashfin. (Musée Stephane Gsell, Algiers).

1111	Death of al-Ghazālī.
1126–1198	Averroes (Ibn Rushd).
1126–1198	Abū Madyan, chief founder of Ṣūfism in North Africa.
1127	Death of Guilhem de Poitiers, the first of the Troubadours.
1147–1269	Almohads.
1156	Death of Peter the Venerable, Abbot of Cluny, who commissioned the first Latin translation of the Qur'ān.
1160	Notre-Dame at Paris.
1162	Death at Seville of the physician Ibn Zuhr.
1166	Death at Baghdad of the great saint Sidi 'Abd al-Qādir al-Jīlānī, chief promoter of the fraternity movement.
1187	Saladin retakes Jerusalem.
1195	Victory of the Almohads at Alarcos.
1198–1216	Innocent III pope.
1198–1250	Frederick II King of Sicily, then Emperor.
1202	Muslims at Benares.
1208	Albigensian Crusade.
1209	St. Francis of Assisi founds his order.
1212	Defeat of the Almohads at Las Navas de Tolosa.
1220	St. Dominic organises his order.
1227	Death of Gengis Khan.
1230	Averroes is translated into Latin.
1235	Death of the great Egyptian mystic poet Ibn al-Fāriḍ.
1240	Death of the great Ṣūfi writer Ibn 'Arabī.
1248	The Christians take Seville.
1257	Hūlāgū exterminates the Assassins.
1257	The Sorbonne.
1258	Hūlāgū takes Baghdad.
1273	Death at Konia of the great Persian mystic poet Jalāl ad-Dīn ar-Rūmī.
1299	Ottoman Turks.
1307–1314	Progress of the Templars.
1405	Death of Tamerlane.
1406	Death of Ibn Khaldūn.
1453	Capture of Constantinople by the Ottomans.
1492	Capture of Grenada by Ferdinand and Isabella. Discovery of America.
1499–1722	Safavids in Persia, Shī'ism the official religion.
1516	The Turks in Algeria.
1530	Death of Babar, founder of the Moghul Empire in India.
1538	Guillaume Postel (1505–1581) nominated Professor of Arabic in the Collège Royal of Francis I.
1542	He publishes the *De orbis terrae concordia* where the Qur'ān is commented on.
1799	Bonaparte in Egypt.

1804	The Wahhābis take Mecca.
1805–1849	Muḥammad 'Ali pasha of Egypt.
1811–1818	He defeats the Wahhābis.
1830	The French at Algiers.
1849	Execution of the Bāb in Persia.
1870	Foundation of the American University of Beirut.
1874	Foundation of the University Saint-Joseph at Beirut.
1883	Death of al-Bustānī, restorer of Arabic literature in the Lebanon.
1905	Death of Muḥammad 'Abduh.
1908	Foundation of the University of Cairo.
1922	Fu'ād I King of Egypt.
1923	Foundation of the University of Damascus.
1924	The Wahhābis take Mecca.
1924	Mustafa Kemal suppresses the caliphate.
1925	The sheikh 'Ali 'Abd ar-Rāziq publishes *Islam and the roots of power*, on the distinction between the spiritual and the temporal.
1926	First Arab works of Taha Hussein.
1926	Ibn Sa'ūd King of the Hijāz.
1931	Death of the Lebanese writer Jibrān Khalīl Jibrān.
1932	Death of the poet Shawqī.
1938	Foundation, by Ḥasan al-Bannā', of the reactionary political and religious movement of the Muslim Brotherhood.
1945	Proclamation of the Indonesian Republic.
1947	Birth of Pakistan.
1947	Statute of Algeria.

NOTE ON THE SPELLING OF ARABIC WORDS

The transliteration of Arabic words and phrases follows the orthodox practice of orientalists, except in the case of one or two everyday words such as "harem" and "Saladin".

SELECT BIBLIOGRAPHY

MUḤAMMAD AND HIS ENVIRONMENT

TOR ANDRAE, *Muhammad, the Man and his Faith* (translated by T. Menzel, London, 1936).
R. BELL, *The Origin of Islam in its Christian Environment* (London, 1926).
RÉGIS BLACHÈRE, *Le problème de Mahomet* (1953).
CAETANI, *Annali dell' Islam* (Milan, 1905–1926, 10 vols).
CAETANI, *Chronographia . . . islamica* (1–922 (622–1517); in fol. 1912, 5 vols.).
CASANOVA, *Mohammed et la fin du monde* (1911).
E. DERMENGHEM, *The Life of Mahomet* (translated by A. Yorke, London, 1930).

Étienne Dinet et Sliman ben Ibrahim, *La vie de Mohammed prophète d'Allah*, s.d.
A. Guillaume, *The Life of Muhammad, being a Translation of the Sirah* (London, 1955).
Haikal, *Hayat Muhammad* (Cairo, 1935).
Hamidullah, *Documents sur la diplomatie musulmane à l'epoque du Prophète et des khalifes orthodoxes;* and *corpus. . . .* (1935).
H. Lammens, *Le Berceau de l'Islam, L'Arabie occidentale à la veille de l'Hegire*, Vol. I: *le Climat, les Bedouins* (Rome, 1914).
H. Lammens, *La Mecque à la veille de l'Hegire* (Beirut, 1924).
Levi della Vida, article *Sira*, in the Encyclopaedia of Islam.
W. Muir, *Life of Mohammad*, ed. by T. H. Weir (Edinburgh, 1923).
D. L. O'Leary, *Arabia before Muhammad* (London, 1927).
A. Sprenger, *Das Leben und die Lehre des Mohammed* (Berlin, 2nd ed., 1869).
W. Montgomery Watt, *Muhammad at Mecca* (Oxford, 1953).
W. Montgomery Watt, *Muhammad at Medina* (Oxford, 1956).

THE QUR'ĀN AND THE ḤADĪTH

A. J. Arberry, *The Koran Interpreted* (London, 1955).
R. Bell, *Translation of the Qur'an* (Edinburgh, 1937–39).
R. Bell, *Introduction to the Qur'an* (Edinburgh, 1943).
Malek Bennabi, *Le phenomène coranique* (Algiers, 1947).
Régis Blachère, *Le Coran, Introduction au Coran* and *Traduction nouvelle* (1947–51, 4 Vols.).
Bokhari, *Les Traditions islamiques* (translated by O. Houdas and W. Marcais, 4 Vols., 1903–14).
N. J. Dawood, *The Koran* (Penguin Books, London, 1955).
I. Goldziher, *Muhammedanische Studien* (Halle, 1888, 1890).
A. Guillaume, *The Traditions of Islam* (Oxford, 1924).
J. Jomier, *Le commentaire coranique du Manar;* Tendances modernes de l'exegese. . . . (1954).
Nöldeke, Schwally, etc. . . . , *Geschichte des Qorans* (Leipzig, 1919).
E. H. Palmer, *The Koran*, various editions.
M. Pickthall, *The Meaning of the Glorious Koran* (London, 1930).
J. M. Rodwell, *The Koran* (London, 1909).

THE EVOLUTION OF ISLAMIC RELIGION AND PHILOSOPHY

J.-M. Abd-el-Jalil, *Aspects intèrieurs de l'Islam* (2nd ed., 1952).
Mohammed Abdouh, *Rissalat al tawhid, Expose de la religion musulmane* (translated by B. Michel and M. Abdel Razik, 1925).

A. J. ARBERRY, *Sufism* (London, 1951).
SIR THOMAS ARNOLD, and ALFRED GUILLAUME, *The Legacy of Islam* (Oxford, 1931).
G. H. BOUSQUET, *L'Islam maghrebin* (1943 and 1955).
C. BROCKLEMANN, *History of the Islamic Peoples* (London, 1949).
C. BROCKELMANN, *Geschichte der arabischen Litteratur* (new edition and supplement, Leyden, 5 Vols., 1937–49).
E. G. BROWNE, *A Literary History of Persia* (4 Vols., 2nd edition, Cambridge, 1928).
ÉMILE DERMENHGEM, *Vies des saints musulmans* (1942).
ÉMILE DERMENGHEM, *Les plus beaux textes arabes* (1951).
ÉMILE DERMENGHEM, *Le culte des saints dans l'Islam maghrebin* (1954).
A. S. DIMAND, *A Handbook of Muhammadan Art* (New York, 1947).
LOUIS GARDET AND MM. ANAWATI, *Introduction à la Theologie musulmane* (1948).
LOUIS GARDET, *La Cite musulmane* (1954).
M. GAUDEFROY-DEMOMBYNES, *Muslim Institutions* (London, 1950).
M. GAUDEFROY-DEMOMBYNES, *Le pèlerinage à La Mekke* (1923).
H. A. R. GIBB, *Modern Trends in Islam* (Chicago, 1947).
H. A. R. GIBB, *The Structure of Religious Thought in Islam* (1948).
H. A. R. GIBB, *Mohammedanism* (London, 1950).
I. GOLDZIHER, *Vorlesungen uber den Islam* (Heidelberg, 1925).
G. E. VON GRUNEBAUM, *Medieval Islam* (Chicago, 1946 and 1953).
L'Islam et l'occident (Cahiers du Sud, 1947).
H. LAMMENS, *Islam* (London).
LACY (DE) O'LEARY, *Arabic Thought and its place in History* (1939).
B. LEWIS, *The Arabs in History* (London, 1950).
GEORGES MARCAIS, *L'art de l'Islam* (1946).
HENRI MASSÉ, *L'islam* (new edition, 1940).
LOUIS MASSIGNON, *La passion d'Al-Hallaj* (1922).
LOUIS MASSIGNON, *Essai sur les origines du lexique technique de la mystique musulmane* (1922 and 1954).
R. A. NICHOLSON, *A Literary History of the Arabs* (2nd edition, Cambridge, 1930).
CH. PELLAT, *Langue et litterature arabe* (1952).
J. SAUVAGET, *Introduction à l'histoire de l'Orient musulman* (1943 and 1946).
JOSEPH SCHACHT, *The Origins of Muhammadan Jurisprudence* (Oxford, 1950).
MARGARET SMITH, *Readings from the Mystics of Islam* (London, 1950).
W. MONTGOMERY WATT, *Free Will and Predestination in Early Islam* (London, 1948).
W. MONTGOMERY WATT, *The Faith and Practice of al-Ghazali* (Oxford, 1952).
A. J. WENSINCK, *The Muslim Creed* (Cambridge, 1932).

G. ANTONIUS, *The Arab Awakening* (London, 1939).
A. J. ARBERRY and R. LANDAU (Eds.,), *Islam Today* (London, 1943).
A. BALAGIJA A., *Les musulmans yougoslaves* (1940).
MALEK BENNABI, *Vocation de l'islam* (1954).
P. CACHIA, *Taha Husayn* (London, 1957).
F. W. FERNAU, *Moslems on the March* (London, 1955).
H. A. R. GIBB (Ed.), *Whither Islam?* (London, 1932).
ALPHONSE GOUILLY, *L'islam en A. O. F.* (1952).
L. LEHURAUX, *Islam et chretiente en Algérie* (1950).
L. MASSIGNON, *Annuaire du monde musulman* (1955).
V. MONTEIL, *Essai sur l'islam en U. R. R. S.* (Revue des Études Islamiques, 1952 and 1953).
A. J. TOYNBEE, *The World and the West* (1953).

Further references in W. A. C. Dobson (Ed.), *A Select List of Books on the Civilizations of the Orient* (Oxford, 1955).

NOTE ON THE ILLUSTRATIONS

Bibliothèque Nationale, pp. 32, 33, 48, 71, 72, 97, 98, 99, 105, 110, 116, 119, 125, 126, 128, 149, 158, 163, 164, 165, 168, 171, 182, 188.
Edinburgh University, pp. 14, 15, 19, 34, 37.
British Museum, pp. 115, 139.
University Press, Oxford, pp. 155, 161, 169, 170.
Musée de l'Homme, Paris, pp. 2, 86, 131.
Musée Stéphane-Gsell, Algiers, p. 185.
E. Dermenghem, pp. 84, 85, 150, 152, 175.
Jean Roman, pp. 57, 58, 59, 137.
Archives Photographiques, pp. 74, 124.
Documentation française, pp. 4, 121.
Office Marocain du Tourisme, p. 132.
Ofalac, p. 69.
Almasy, pp. 31, 39.
Roger-Viollet, pp. 78, 83, 89.
Vie Catholique Illustrée, pp. 24, 79.
Anderson-Giraudon, p. 184.
Roger Roche, pp. 7, 8, 9, 45, 52, 55, 90, 92, 100, 108.

[LONGMANS], GREEN AND CO LTD
[6 & 7 CLIFFOR]D STREET LONDON W 1

THIBAULT HOUSE THIBAULT SQUARE CAPE TOWN
605–611 LONSDALE STREET MELBOURNE C 1

LONGMANS, GREEN AND CO INC
55 FIFTH AVENUE NEW YORK 3

LONGMANS, GREEN AND CO
20 CRANFIELD ROAD TORONTO 16

ORIENT LONGMANS PRIVATE LTD
CALCUTTA BOMBAY MADRAS
DELHI HYDERABAD DACCA

HARPER AND BROTHERS
49 EAST 33RD STREET
NEW YORK 16

First published in France
by Editions du Seuil, Paris

This English edition first published 1958

TYPE SET BY WESTERN PRINTING SERVICES LTD., BRISTOL
PRINTED IN GREAT BRITAIN BY LOWE AND BRYDONE (PRINTERS) LTD.